Motivationals for

MOM

Motivationals for
MOM

Inspiring You to Be All You Can Be

Chrys Howard

Bestselling author of Hugs for Daughters

HOWARD BOOKS
A DIVISION OF SIMON & SCHUSTER
New York   London   Toronto   Sydney

Our purpose at Howard Books is to:
Increase faith in the hearts of growing Christians
Inspire holiness in the lives of believers
Instill hope in the hearts of struggling people everywhere
Because He's coming again!

Published by Howard Books, a division of Simon & Schuster, Inc.
1230 Avenue of the Americas, New York, NY 10020
www.howardpublishing.com

HOWARD
BOOKS

Motivationals for Mom © 2008 by Chrys Howard

Library of Congress Cataloging-in-Publication Data

Howard, Chrys, 1953–
  Motivationals for mom : inspiring you to be all you can be / Chrys Howard.
    p. cm.
1. Mothers—Religious life. 2. Christian women—Religious life. I.
Title.
  BV4529.18.H68 2008
  248.8'431—dc22

2008026195

ISBN: 978-1-4516-6567-3

10 9 8 7 6 5 4 3 2 1

HOWARD and colophon are registered trademarks of Simon & Schuster, Inc.

Manufactured in the United States of America

For information regarding special discounts for bulk purchases, please contact: Simon & Schuster Special Sales at 1-800-456-6798 or business@simonandschuster.com.

Edited by Between the Lines
Cover design by Left Coast Design
Interior design by Stephanie D. Walker

This book is dedicated to every mom
who sacrifices a more convenient lifestyle
to love and care for her children.

To every mom who stays up late at night worrying
about a sick child, a homework assignment,
or the bully down the street and
every mom who prays for the safety of her child
away at war or on a mission field.

There is no tougher job, no greater challenge,
no higher calling than being called "mom."

Thank you for answering the call.

Contents

Contents

Actions

The good, the right, the true—these are the actions
appropriate for daylight hours.
Figure out what will please Christ, and then do it.
Ephesians 5:9

Read It

"Actions speak louder than words." Perhaps you remember hearing that admonition from your mother. Perhaps you say those words to your children. The saying has lasted through generations because it's true—our actions communicate, both positively and negatively.

Nothing soothes a crying baby like a mother's comforting arms, and nothing tells an eleven-year-old boy that you adore him like hugging him tightly even as he tries to wrestle away. Those are two obvious examples, but even our more subtle actions speak no less loudly. Body language speaks volumes to our husbands, our children, and everyone around us.

I love how *The Message* states this important principle: "Figure out what will please Christ, and then do it." So today, do just that. Watch yourself for one twenty-four-hour period and see what language your body speaks. Be alert to the facial expressions and reactions you get from your family—they're good indicators of whether you're sending the signals you really want to send.

I'll admit, some stern body language can be extremely useful—like during long Sunday sermons, when the kids are restless and your available disciplinary tactics are limited to a "look" and a quiet snap. But it's the other times I'm talking about—the angry look on your face, the hands on the hips, the silent treatment, those types of things. Search your heart and discover what's behind the body language, then address that concern. You'll feel much better when you do, and you will please not only God but also your family . . . and even yourself.

Think It

> *Action and feeling go together;*
> *and by regulating the action, which is*
> *under the more direct control of the will,*
> *we can regulate the feeling, which is not.*
> *William James*

Live It

- Next time you're watching television, turn down the volume and see what you can pick up about people and situations just by observing their body language. Or try watching family videos and studying yourself. What is your body language and demeanor communicating to those you love? Is that what you intend to communicate? What can you change to be more positive and encouraging?

- Be aware of what various postures or mannerisms communicate:

Negatives

- Folding your arms suggests disinterest, skepticism, standoffishness, or hostility.

- Holding your upper arms with your hands indicates defensiveness, not buying in.

- Propping your head on your hands indicates boredom or disinterest.

- Turning your body away from someone indicates stress or a strained relationship.

- Touching your nose while talking indicates discomfort or slight dishonesty.

- Drumming your fingers or rolling your eyes indicates impatience, condescension, displeasure.

Positives

- Unfolding your arms indicates openness, positive feelings.

- Holding or stroking the chin without resting the elbows as a prop indicates concentration, thoughtfulness.

- Turning your body toward a person shows comfort with that person.

- Making and maintaining eye contact (without being menacing) while someone talks communicates interest and support.

- Smiling, a true smile that includes the eyes, goes a long way toward communicating warmth, acceptance, and affection.

2

$\mathcal{A}$mbition

First thing in the morning, she dresses for work,
rolls up her sleeves, eager to get started.
Proverbs 31:17

$\mathcal{R}$ead It

Ambition is an interesting word. "Lacking ambition" is a phrase often used to describe a young man or woman who can't seem to find direction in life. The word *ambitious* means to be determined, motivated, or even pushy.

We worry about children who lack ambition, thinking they'll underperform in life. But we also worry about the child who is too ambitious, concerned that he or she will sacrifice ethics for achievement.

The reality is that a healthy amount of ambition is needed for all of us to succeed in life. As a young child I was shy, and for many years I just followed my more ambitious older sister around and did what she did. My parents even nicknamed me "Me-too," because that's what I said when my sister said anything. They must have wondered if I had an ounce of individual ambition. But as I grew older, I realized that God had a plan for my life, and it wasn't to follow my older sister around. It did require me to become more determined, more motivated, and even "pushy" in a positive way. The result has been a life filled with challenges and many opportunities to touch the lives of others.

As moms, it's so easy to let our children's ambitions ride in the front seat while we strap ours safely in the backseat until the kids are grown. But God desires that we be ambitious too. He wants us to set attainable goals in every area of life—home, career, and church—because when we pursue and achieve them, we *and* our families reap the rewards.

Give yourself permission to set a goal that doesn't involve your kids. Get ambitious, and embrace the adventure!

Think It

The ambitious climbs up high and
perilous stairs, and never cares how to come down;
the desire of rising hath swallowed up his fear of a fall.
Thomas Adams

Live It

Rate yourself. How ambitious are you?

I am a total doormat.	1	2	3	4	5	Stay out of my way if you don't want to get mowed down.

Be honest: How would these other people rate you on the same scale? Your best friend? Your husband? Your kids? Your coworkers?

- If your ambitions and needs are often in conflict with those of others, write down both yours and theirs. Give each a rating from 1 (low priority) to 10 (high priority). Then don't feel guilty about not taking your daughter to the seventh store in a quest to find nail polish that's just a little hotter pink (a 2, even if she swears it's an 11) so you can stop by the auto mechanic's and check on that part that's dragging on the ground and producing sparks as you drive (at least a 7).

- What's one goal you've always talked about achieving but haven't yet acted on? What's one practical step you can take today toward accomplishing that goal?

3

Anger

Go ahead and be angry. You do well to be
angry—but don't use your anger as fuel for revenge.
And don't stay angry. Don't go to bed angry.
Don't give the Devil that kind of foothold in your life.
Ephesians 4:26–27

Read It

I love Ephesians 4:26–27 for two reasons. First, it lets me know that I do have permission to be angry; and second, it gives me boundaries within which to allow those emotions.

As moms, we love the word *boundaries*. When our children first learn to crawl, we mark boundaries with pillows, a chair, or anything stronger than a six-month-old. As they get older, we set new boundaries: "No, you cannot ride with him" or "I'm not kidding, if you leave this house . . ."

But setting boundaries for others is one thing. Setting them for ourselves is another. Back to the subject of anger. Yes, you have the right to be angry when hubby forgets the milk that he promised he would not forget or when little Johnny says "You're not the boss of me." In fact, it's important to get angry sometimes. Anger moves us to action that is necessary on many occasions. However, this verse clearly tells us that we don't have the right to sin

8

when we're angry and gives us the boundaries necessary for appropriate anger. Our anger should not overflow into hate and never, under any circumstances, into abuse. So here's the thing to watch for: Are you losing control when you're angry? If so, stop what you're doing and either walk away or count to ten or twenty. Ask yourself, why am I so angry, and how can I fix the situation?

To think we will never get angry is nonsense, but we can control how we act when we're angry. Don't let anger be the boss of you. Take charge of it!

Think It

A man is about as big as the thing that makes him angry.
Winston Churchill

Live It

- Think back over the past several days. What sorts of things anger you? What does that say about you?

- How do you handle anger—both the little things and those that really set you off. Make a specific plan in advance, outlining how you will react when you get angry—and stick to it. Anger doesn't have to overwhelm you. Resolve that you'll control it, not the other way around.

- Let's face it, our kids know how to push our buttons. Few people can make us angrier than our children can. But if we let them dictate our responses, that gives them control over us and can be destructive both to us and to our relationships. Identify those "buttons" that invariably make you blow. Now, while you're calm, thoughtful, and prayerful, what's a better way to respond? What is your child actually trying to accomplish when he or she pushes that button? How can you address the real issue rather than exploding and rushing down a rabbit trail of anger?

Appearance

4

*Her clothes are well-made and elegant,
and she always faces tomorrow with a smile.*
Proverbs 31:25

Read It

My mother had the most unique ability to put on a hat and some red lipstick and look like she'd walked right off the set of a movie. Mom was tall and slender and had a commanding presence. A hat and red lipstick was all she needed to finish her "glamour mom" look. I was so proud to walk into church with her leading our family of six children. Not until many years later, when I was a mom myself, did I learn what that hat and red lipstick really represented.

You see, glamour was actually the furthest thing from Mom's mind. After dressing six children—five of us within a six-year age bracket—those two accessories were the quickest and easiest way for Mom to look, as she said, "halfway decent."

I'm inspired by the thought of my mom forgoing perhaps a shower or an extra ten minutes of teasing her hair to take care of my siblings and me. But I also love that she respected herself enough to want her appearance to be pleasing. God doesn't care what style of clothes we wear or even if they match; but I believe God does care that we love ourselves enough to present ourselves confidently and so our families are proud to be with us. This can be achieved in the simplest of ways—eating properly, dressing neatly, brushing our hair, or just putting on lipstick and a hat. These simple acts tell your family that they are important enough for you to put your best foot forward for them; and it teaches them that everyone deserves to look his or her best.

That's not a bad reminder for us moms, either.

If you're unhappy with something about your appearance, change it. A new haircut, a free makeover at the mall, a few lost pounds—you're in control. And you really are worth it.

Think It

Keeping your clothes well pressed
will keep you from looking hard pressed.
Coleman Cox

Live It

- Think of one person whose appearance you particularly admire. What are several things that set her above others? Study her look. What's one thing you can emulate to better your own appearance?

- Is it time for a new hairstyle? If you're wearing

your hair the same way you were ten years ago, it's probably time for a change. Go to the mall or a place with crowds, and "people-watch." When you see someone whose hair you really like, ask her who her stylist is (she'll be flattered and feel better about herself too!). Then make an appointment. Seek the stylist's advice, trust his or her expertise, and come home a new and improved you.

- Take a few minutes for you. Page through fashion magazines. Watch TLC's *What Not to Wear*. Notice the styles featured in ads for shoes and eyeglasses, and update your look. Give older items to a charity so someone else can feel better about how she looks too.

- Write down what you like best about your appearance. Then brainstorm one or two ways to make the most of these positives to look your very best.

5

Attitude

Since Jesus went through everything you're going through and more, learn to think like him. Think of your sufferings as a weaning from that old sinful habit of always expecting to get your own way. Then you'll be able to live out your days free to pursue what God wants instead of being tyrannized by what you want.

1 Peter 4:1–2

Read It

I remember my mom saying to one of us six kids, when we were young and obviously unhappy about something, "Get a smile on your face." When I became a mom, I also said those words. Perhaps you've said them as well—or something similar. I also remember my dad saying "Straighten up" to any child who seemed sullen for no reason. As a parent, I've said those words too. Both admonitions are attempts to get children to adopt a better attitude. But of all the things my parents said to persuade me to behave in a better way, what influenced me most wasn't their words; it was the attitude they themselves displayed in times of adversity.

Many times I've witnessed my parents receiving bad news or encountering unpleasant circumstances and responding with a positive spirit and a God-honoring approach.

Life is like a roller-coaster ride. No sooner is your stomach back in place after one big dive than you're plunging down the next one. How can we possibly be expected to keep a good attitude when life seems so uncertain? And what does having a good attitude mean, anyway?

Attitude is the way we think or feel about someone or something, and attitudes can be positive, negative, or neutral. But usually our attitude doesn't confine itself to our feelings. Often it seeps into our behavior, and that's where we need to be careful. Your child may not like green beans, and that's fine, but he's not allowed to throw them against the wall. As we mature, we learn to modify our behavior—when's the last time you flung your dinner across the room? But our actions aren't the only things that should mature—our attitudes should too.

God wants more than our behavior to change; He wants our hearts to change. It isn't enough to just act right; God wants us to think right.

In his letter, the apostle Peter plainly says that Jesus went through every kind of difficulty we could ever go through. I know it's hard to imagine Jesus going through the trials we moms go through. First of all, He never sat up and worried about a sick child.

Wait . . . what about Lazarus?

But He never had to worry about putting food on the table when money is short.

Oh yeah . . . He did feed five thousand people with nothing more than a few fish and some bread.

But surely He never faced the challenges of dealing with His kids' different personalities.

True . . . but not only did He have to deal with twelve very unique personalities chosen to follow Him; He also had to get them to work together to lead others to Him.

Life is not easy, but with a few attitude adjustments, not only will it be more enjoyable, you'll also be able to show others how God can work in their lives by letting them see how He is working in yours.

Think It

*Nothing can stop the man with the right
mental attitude from achieving his goal; nothing
on earth can help the man with the wrong mental attitude.*
Thomas Jefferson

Live It

- Make a list of things in your life that trouble, discourage, or worry you. Now, for each one, write down at least one opportunity, silver lining, or potential for growth it represents. Every time you find yourself worrying this week, pull out your list and think about it from the flip side. Notice how your attitude improves and how much better you feel.

- Think of a positive friend who always makes you feel better and brighter. When you're struggling with a bad attitude, try to spend a little time with her. Resolve to be such an attitude-lifter for others.

- Check your face in a mirror. What attitude does it reflect? Now change your expression to show a happier attitude. How does your face change? Can you feel your attitude and inner well-being changing as well?

6

Beauty

*What matters is not your outer appearance—the styling
of your hair, the jewelry you wear, the cut of your
clothes—but your inner disposition.*
1 Peter 3:4

Read It

The saying "Pretty is as pretty does" echoes a truth that
has been recognized for thousands of years. Physical
beauty doesn't hold a candle to inner beauty.

No matter how nicely we're dressed or made up, we
moms can look pretty awful when we yell and scream at
our children or when we give our husbands that "I can't
believe you left him in the diaper all night!" look. On the
other hand, without a speck of makeup but clothed with a
kind and gentle spirit, we can show others, especially our
family, that beauty truly is more than skin deep.

The day-to-day responsibility of raising kids is the
hardest job you'll ever do. No employee is capable of
making you madder than a twelve-year-old with a smart
mouth does. But resist the urge to let your "ugly" out.
Remain calm and handle the situation with firmness but
also with gentleness.

The next time your husband ignores the trash can
until adding just one more French fry would cause it to
topple over, show him that your beauty isn't just on your

face—it goes all the way down to your heart. Give him a hug and a compliment, and see if the trash doesn't get taken out shortly afterward.

What inner "clothes" are you wearing today? Make sure you give more careful attention to them than you do to the clothes in your closet.

Think It

Though we travel the world over to find the beautiful,
we must carry it with us or we will find it not.
Ralph Waldo Emerson

Live It

• Take time for a beauty makeover—inside and out. While your facial is exfoliating or that conditioner does its stuff on your hair, while doing your nails or soaking in a moisturizing bath, use the time to focus on your inner beauty. Pray, meditate, or read the Bible or an inspiring book. What steps can you take to become a woman of true inner beauty?

• How much time each day do you spend on your beauty routine—hair, makeup, nails, teeth whiteners, etc.? Really, don't just guess—clock it. Commit to spending at least an equal amount of time daily on cultivating your inner beauty.

7

Beliefs

The gullible believe anything they're told;
the prudent sift and weigh every word.
Proverbs 14:15

Read It

Sometimes it seems most of our energy is spent trying to get a hot meal on the table instead of out of a bag, or keeping the kids from killing each other. But in the quiet hours of the night, what we lose sleep over is whether we're doing enough to pass on our spiritual beliefs. In a recent Focus on the Family survey, spiritual training was reported as one of the top three areas where parents want help.

We all want our children to grow up strong in the Lord and to have an everlasting home in heaven. How can we ensure that happens? We can't.

Wow, that's not what you wanted to hear, is it? But it's true. As children grow, they will not always make the choices we want them to make. God's children don't always act as He wants them to, and ours won't either. However, we can take steps to help guide our children to want to follow God.

First of all, without making your children crazy with "the Bible this" and "the Bible that," you can use everyday experiences such as homework, sports, mealtimes, and games to teach biblical principles. You can also strive to make your home environment Christlike. Speak God's Word to your children, but remember that if you don't live in a way that's consistent with your words, you're sending mixed signals and your children will be confused about right and wrong behavior.

Another good practice is to verbally pass down family traditions of faith. Say words like, "Your grandfather loved God and always put Him first." (Of course, only say things that are true.) If you're the first person of faith in your family, then speak personally. A tradition handed down for only one generation is still a tradition, and your children can pass it to their children, further establishing the legacy. Traditions of faith can also help your kids develop their identity and strengthen their character by giving them tools for right behavior—a code for living.

Finally, pray like crazy! Seek God's help daily, both individually and as a family. Doing these things will go a long way toward making sure you and your children hold to—and live by—what you believe.

Think It

If you don't have solid beliefs, you cannot build a stable life.
Beliefs are like the foundation of a building,
and they are the foundation to build your life upon.
Alfred A. Montapert

Live It

- Have family devotions with your children—daily is great, but at least once a week. These don't have to be long and drawn out. Keep them simple. Help the kids see how the Bible applies to the issues and problems they face every day. Discuss dilemmas and situations you are facing yourself so they can see how you put your beliefs and faith into action.

- If you don't have a family Bible with your family's history recorded, start one this week. Get the kids involved in researching and collecting family history and key spiritual stories and traditions.

- How did your family pass on their beliefs to you? What can you learn—both positive and negative— from their examples that will help you with your own children?

8

Busyness

She's up before dawn, preparing breakfast
for her family and organizing her day.
Proverbs 31:15

Read It

Who doesn't think they're busy? Everyone does. It's the nature of our society in today's world. I can remember when computers first came on the scene for personal use. My brother was on the cutting edge of the revolution and still teaches computer science on a high-school level. One of the first things he tells his students is that computers were not invented to save people time, as many people think, but to make their work more efficient.

It seems we're all looking for ways to save time. Time is our most valuable commodity. If we can't change the amount of time we have, we have to try to work more efficiently. We also want to be sure our busyness is productive and God-honoring. Does that mean getting up while it's still dark, as this verse suggests? I hope not! I know some strong, faithful believers who love to sleep in.

As moms, we need to assess the needs of our families and be sure the activities we spend our days involved in are ones that promote a healthy family and please our heavenly Father. Shopping, eating out, exercising, and spending time with friends are all important parts of life, but they should be carefully balanced with working, serving others, helping our children, spending time with our husbands, and cultivating our spiritual life.

Balancing your daily schedule can be harder than balancing a baby on one hip and the phone on your shoulder while you fry an egg. Here are a few helpful hints: Keep a calendar book or a family calendar in your kitchen. Post a magnetic notepad on your refrigerator to write down necessary items for shopping trips. Spend a few minutes every evening reviewing your to-do list for tomorrow. Those few minutes can mean the difference between a stress-free, productive day and a day that makes you want to pull your hair out.

Today's women are sometimes criticized for taking on too much and being too busy. God loves a busy woman—He just wants the busyness to be of value. Take some time to look carefully at your schedule and be sure you've included the right amount of important busyness.

Think It

*Every man is worth just so much
as the things are worth
about which he busies himself.*
Marcus Aurelius Antoninus

Live It

- If you're feeling too busy to play with your kids, really talk with your husband, or spend time reading the Bible or praying, read Luke 10:38–42. How do your priorities compare with Martha's?

- What's your biggest time-waster? Give it up for one week and see how good you feel about what you accomplish.

- Check the balance in your life. Draw a line down the center of a piece of paper. Label one side "Urgent" (for items with pressing deadlines, like paying bills, walking the dog, baking cookies for school, cleaning the house for company) and the other "Important" (for tasks with long-term consequences—activities that are an investment in the lives of our children and others). Decide in which column each task that is making you feel too busy belongs. Resolve to give priority to those things that are truly important, not just those that clamor loudest for your attention.

- Learn to delegate. Concentrate on what you're good at and love doing. Find ways to delegate other tasks. Who knows, you might find that while cooking is a chore for you, one of your children is a budding chef who finds it a creative delight!

9

Character

What this adds up to, then, is this: no more lies,
no more pretense. Tell your neighbor the truth.
In Christ's body we're all connected to each other, after all.
When you lie to others, you end up lying to yourself.
Ephesians 4:25

Read It

A good bit of attention has been given to the word
character in the last few decades. It seems the world has
decided that character doesn't really count in such areas as
politics, entertainment, and media. But the Bible makes
it clear that character *does* count, and as moms we really
take this to heart.

Yet even the definition of *character* seems an ironic
paradox: it can mean "the behavior typical of someone or
a group," or it can mean "moral strength"—not always the
same thing. So there is a tiny bit of pressure on us to put
a face to the "moral strength" part and to let our children
witness it clearly. They won't likely get a positive example
of character from a TV show or a video game; they need
to see it in people they love and trust.

But the group-behavior meaning of character isn't
all bad. Since you are reading this book, you probably
identify yourself with the group defined as "Christian

families." What does that mean? Well, it means that your family makes up a group, and your group's behavior is its character. So, as a Christian family, it means that when the neighbor isn't nice, you're nice anyway. It means when the cashier rings up one gallon of milk and you got two, you bring that to his or her attention and pay for both gallons. It means that anytime you have the opportunity to react with honesty, integrity, and respect, you do.

Children love to catch their parents doing the right thing. It gives them a sense of security that all is right in their world. The days are long gone when Mom, Dad, Grandma, and Grandpa were the only influencers in a child's life. The old farmhouse situated miles away from the nearest neighbor rarely exists today. Even if it does, it's probably well equipped with an Internet connection, PlayStation, and multiple TVs. Now more than ever, children need to see moms doing the right thing. So, as you're teaching your children to count to one hundred, remember to also teach them to count on you to show them what true character is.

Think It

Personality can open doors,
but only character can keep them open.
Elmer G. Letterman

Live It

- Live your life as if someone is always watching. They are. Think about what defines who you really are. What are the rules to live by that you'd like to pass on to your children? What are some practical ways you can demonstrate these ideals and live them out as your children watch you? Remember, anything it costs you to live a life of character rather than taking the easy or convenient way is just a small investment in your children's future that will pay big dividends.

- When you find an example of good character in a television or movie character or in a book you're enjoying together, point it out. Discuss it. Applaud it. Let your children know that this is the kind of behavior and character you admire and expect from them. And when you see evidence of good character in your kids' lives, acknowledge it and commend them. Tell them you're proud. They'll do it again and again.

Courage

*So, my dear Christian friends, companions in following
this call to the heights, take a good hard look at Jesus.
He's the centerpiece of everything we believe, faithful in
everything God gave him to do. Moses was also faithful,
but Jesus gets far more honor. A builder is more valuable
than a building any day. Every house has a builder,
but the Builder behind them all is God. Moses did a
good job in God's house, but it was all servant work,
getting things ready for what was to come. Christ as
Son is in charge of the house. Now, if we can only keep
a firm grip on this bold confidence, we're the house!*

Hebrews 3:1 6

Read It

I love the cowardly lion in the movie *The Wizard of Oz*. His
desire to be courageous fights with his nature to be timid.
Biographers have described the man who played the
character the same way. You may remember one of the
songs from the movie, where the lion sang with a shaky
voice "If I only had the nerve." Do you sometimes wish
you "only had the nerve"?

Being a mom is not a job for cowards, as you well know.
It's a job that requires courage every day. It's brave to just
hold a six-pound infant, much less place his slippery little

body in a tub of warm water. Many strong, courageous men shy away from that! Yet sometimes we moms lack the courage we need to stand up with strength and boldness when our children are no longer six-pound babies.

It takes courage to deal with the tough situations in life—to tell Satan "No! I will not let you have my child." But you can do it! Start when your children are young, and take strong stands against sin and against allowing your children to be involved in situations that may compromise their faith. Practice by role-playing with them, showing them how they can be bold and courageous when others try to lead them down the wrong path.

Before long, you and they will realize that, just as the cowardly lion discovered, courage is already inside you— because God put it there. You don't have to travel the yellow brick road; simply walk hand in hand with Jesus.

Think It

Courage is what it takes to stand up and speak;
courage is also what it takes to sit down and listen.
Winston Churchill

Live It

- Read a biography about a believer (or simply Google him or her) who showed great courage. Consider Eric Liddell, Corrie ten Boom, Brother

Andrew, Martin Luther, Fanny Crosby, William Wilberforce, George Washington Carver, Florence Nightingale, Helen Roseveare, Martin and Gracia Burnham, Dennis Byrd, and Jim Elliot.

- What turns you into a "Cowardly Lion"? Don't avoid it or run from it. Turn and face it head-on. Talk to your daughter about why her clothes smelled like marijuana. Check your son's computer if you have suspicions about what he's been doing on it. Call the doctor about that nagging symptom you've been hoping will go away on its own. Fears and problems, like shadows, only seem bigger as the sun sinks lower. When we shine light on a problem, the shadows flee and we see that our problems are not as big and scary as we imagined.

II

Difficulties

*Anyone who meets a testing challenge head-on and manages
to stick it out is mighty fortunate. For such persons loyally
in love with God, the reward is life and more life.*

James 1:12

Read It

Some of you may not be far removed from the test-taking
days of school. For others it's been a while, but I'm sure
you remember that sinking feeling you had as the teacher
passed out a test you hadn't studied for. I certainly do. But
do you also remember the power you felt when a test was
placed on your desk and you knew the answer to each and
every question? What was the difference between those
two situations? Most likely, some of the difference lay in
your preparation.

Whatever age you are, by now you know that life is a
series of tests. Some are like those difficult, fill-in-the-
blank tests: you have to know exactly what to do, without
any clues or help at all. Instant recall is the name of that
game. Others are like the matching or multiple choice
tests: the answers are there somewhere, but seeing them
all mixed up can be confusing and make you uncertain
which to choose.

The difference between real life and a test at school
is that in life, we rarely have a study guide to follow or

32

a notebook with answers at our fingertips. Life is filled with too many unexpected events, especially where children are concerned, to sum up all the information we need in one notebook. Just when we think everything is going smoothly, someone gets sick, the school calls, a fight breaks out, or worse. As children of God and as moms with a purpose, we have to be prepared for these difficult days. But how do you get ready for that kind of test?

One simple step is to recognize that difficulties are a part of life. The goal of acknowledging this isn't to make you look toward the future with despair but rather to help you be prepared mentally when you have to face tough times head-on. God has made us an awesome promise: He tells us that if we persevere—if we do our part to prepare and hang on through the difficulties in life—He will give us what we need in order to pass the test with flying colors.

Think It

There are two ways of meeting difficulties: you alter the difficulties, or you alter yourself to meet them.
Phyllis Bottome

Live It

- Think about and make a plan to help you prepare now for the possibility of difficult days to come in the following areas:

- Lean financial times
- Severe weather/prolonged electrical outage
- House fire
- Flu pandemic
- Retirement/aging
- Medical emergency
- Death of a loved one
- Deterioration, aging of home/automobile
- Relationship strains
- Legal problems
- Auto accident
- Threat of terrorism

- If you don't ve one, start a "rainy day" fund.

- Memorize some of the following Bible verses, before you need them in a time of crisis:
  - Genesis 28:15
  - Proverbs 3:5
  - Isaiah 26:33
  - Isaiah 43:2
  - Isaiah 50:10
  - John 16:33
  - Romans 8:35–37
  - 1 Corinthians 10:13

Disappointments

Be content with who you are, and don't put on airs. God's strong hand is on you; he'll promote you at the right time. Live carefree before God; he is most careful with you.

1 Peter 5:7

Read It

Disappointments are part of life, for the toddler who doesn't get the candy in Mom's purse, the college student who can't get in the "fun" teacher's class, or the working mom whose promotion hopes don't materialize. Learning to live with disappointment is something every human being must do in order to function in life.

Those disappointments are tough enough, but we also sometimes have to deal with disappointments in our relationships. Though we love them and they love us, still at times our husbands and children disappoint us. Expectations run high as wedding bells chime and birth announcements are sent. But as time goes on, our expectations and our experiences sometimes don't match up. Spouses aren't always nice to each other. Kids make poor decisions. One way or another, we let each other down.

God knows this will happen. It happened to Him.

His hopes that Adam and Eve would live in close relationship with Him in a garden especially designed to bless them didn't exactly work out. His chosen and beloved servant Moses disrespected Him and disqualified himself from enjoying the beautiful Promised Land God had prepared in Canaan.

But talk about turning lemons into lemonade. God is the ultimate lemonade maker. He still spoke directly with Moses, and He led him to a mountaintop where he could see the land the Israelites were about to enter before he died. And as for the relational chasm created by Adam and Eve, God bridged that gap by sending His own Son so that all of humanity could enjoy restored fellowship with Him.

God didn't wallow in His disappointment at the hands of those He loved. He turned those situations around by doing something good.

Rick Warren, in his book *The Purpose-Driven Life*, advises us not to waste our pain. Instead, we should take our disappointments and heartaches and use them to bring God glory and to do good for others.

Are you feeling disappointed? Open your eyes to ways you can turn your situation around to do good and glorify God. Your example will be noticed by little eyes and ears that depend on you to show them the way.

Think It
Now is no time to think of what you do not have.
Think of what you can do with what there is.
Ernest Hemingway

Live It

- Make fresh-squeezed lemonade as a special treat for your family. For each lemon you squeeze, imagine a disappointment you're facing or have endured. As you squeeze the lemon, think of a way to "make lemonade"—make something good out of the situation. Thank God for the good He has, can, or will bring from it.

- Remembering how we've disappointed God and others can make us more understanding and forgiving when others disappoint us. When you pray, remember Christ's example in the Lord's Prayer: "Forgive us our sins, as we forgive those who sin against us" (Luke 11:4 NLT).

- Read Romans 5:3–5 with your children. How does this passage give hope? Discuss some ways God has brought good from the disappointments in your lives.

13

Discipline

*If you love learning, you love
the discipline that goes with it—
how shortsighted to refuse correction!*
Proverbs 12:1

Read It

Understanding the importance of discipline is half the battle in living a disciplined life. Many people don't understand that discipline is the surest way to achieve the success they desire.

If you're a stay-at-home mom, sometimes it's tough to discipline yourself to get up and moving. The housework piles up and, no matter what you do, it never goes away. And if you work outside the home, you're in a constant struggle to "do it all," leaving you exhausted and with too many things still undone.

Don't save discipline for your children—we all need it, even moms. Being disciplined simply means being in control or having things in order. If you feel out of control, maybe you just need a little discipline. The good and the bad of the situation is, it's all up to you. There's no "other" mother around to wake you up after the snooze button is pressed for the third time. No drill sergeant yelling at you to make your bed or do your sit-ups. But you can do it! Lay out a plan to become better disciplined. Tackle it like you do any other job: start with just one thing. Once you've conquered that one thing, you'll be able to say, "If I can to that, then I can do the next thing."

Before you know it, you'll feel better about yourself and your household will run like a well-oiled machine.

Think It

If we don't discipline ourselves, the world will do it for us.
William Feather

Live It

- Make a list of things you need to do. Resolve to do just one today, no matter how much you'd rather run away or take a nap. Do that one thing, cross it off your list, and you might be surprised to find you feel inspired to keep going and tackle another.

- You can do anything for just one week. Commit to live a more disciplined life for just seven days, and see how you like the results.

- Find an accountability partner. Offer each other encouragement and support while you each strive to bring discipline to your lives. Get together at least once a week (in person or by phone or e-mail) to discuss your efforts and progress. Sometimes just knowing someone will be checking in on us is enough to keep us on track.

14

Dreams

Don't for a minute envy
careless rebels; soak yourself in the
Fear-of-GOD—That's where your future lies.
Then you won't be left with an armload of nothing.
Proverbs 23:17–18

Read It

I'm soaking in a hot tub with bubbles up to my chin. The glow from the candles gives the perfect amount of light for me to read my book, but I can hardly keep my eyes open to read because the soft sounds of music playing are lulling me to sleep.

Then, as the saying goes, I woke up.

Dreaming is such a pleasant way to escape the realities of life. I look at it as a vacation in my sleep, a fantasy world. But not all dreams are mere fantasy. Often what we call dreams are our really fondest hopes. The scene I just imagined was certainly a fond hope of mine when my three children were small—but sometimes I feared it would never become a reality.

As moms, many times our dreams and our realities do not match up. Life is seldom as pleasant or as easy as what we hope for. That's why they're called dreams. When your sweet husband proposed to you, your dream did not include the night he forgot your birthday and made plans to play cards with his buddies. The day you discovered you were pregnant, your dream did not include the night your teenager didn't come home and you frantically called friends and hospitals looking for him.

No, our dreams are not full of things hurtful or harmful. We call those nightmares.

Did you know that God has hopes and dreams for you? He wants good for you, not evil. And the best part is, if we keep our hearts on the right path, always moving closer to Him, what God dreams for us *can* become reality.

Dreams can be a nice little escape. But be careful that you don't spend too much time daydreaming and not enough time attending to the real-life dreams God wants you to pursue.

Think It
Keep your eyes on the stars, and your feet on the ground.
Theodore Roosevelt

Live It

- It's tempting to dream about good things in the future. But don't overlook the present good. Think of a few things in your life that are fulfillments of earlier dreams, or maybe even unexpected gifts you never even dreamed possible. Thank God for them.

- When your life turns into the occasional nightmare, instead of despairing, look at the flip side. What "dream" are you living (having a healthy family, owning a nice home) that is being overshadowed by the nightmare (a willful daughter, a roof that leaks)? Focus on the dream fulfilled, and you won't feel quite so sorry for yourself.

- Share one secret dream with a trusted friend or confidante. Discuss what you might do to make a worthwhile dream come true.

15

Emotions

A sound mind makes for a robust body,
but runaway emotions corrode the bones.
Proverbs 14:30

Read It

Looking for more energy? For a strong body? Forget dietary supplements and health clubs, look for it inside yourself!

Well, don't totally forget vitamins and exercise—we all need those. But much of the battle for a more satisfying life takes place in our hearts and heads—in the struggle to control our emotions.

Romans 8:6 (NIV) tells us that "the mind controlled by the Spirit is life and peace." I know, some of you are saying, "I can't help it—I'm just an emotional person. I cry or yell a lot." Since when did "I can't help it" become a good excuse for anything? You probably don't accept that justification from your children when they misbehave. While it may be true that some people's natural temperament tends toward more emotional responses, we can, with the help of God's Spirit, bring our emotions under control.

When my children were growing up and tried to use the "I can't help it" defense, I often answered, "So if I gave you a hundred dollars to behave right now, you're telling me you couldn't earn that hundred?" That was usually all it took to get them to realize they could indeed control their emotions—they were simply choosing not to.

Sure, it's easier to fly off the handle than it is to control your temper. But the internal turmoil you're likely to feel afterward—or to cause in others—isn't good for your health and can be even more destructive to your heart. If you're feeling a little out of control, sit down today and take an inventory of your emotions. Evaluate yourself as though you were a boss evaluating an employee. How would you rate yourself in this area? If you're coming up a little short, make some changes today. If $100 isn't enough to help you control your emotions, give yourself a raise. Learn to creatively handle the situations you face and keep your emotions in check. Stay healthy by staying in control.

Think It

*The appearance of things
change according to the emotions,
and thus we see magic and beauty in them,
while the magic and beauty are really in ourselves.*
Kahlil Gibran

Live It

- Keep an emotional diary this week. It can be as simple as tracking your feelings each morning or evening by jotting down one word, a brief description, a little smiley face or emoticon, or anything that captures your current mood. What surprises you when you see it in print?

- What makes your emotions more volatile? What makes them easier to control? Not getting enough sleep and eating poorly can make us feel emotionally fragile. So can hormonal changes in our bodies. You might find that getting proper nutrition, adding soy to your diet (it mimics estrogen), getting an extra hour of sleep, or taking time out for a cup of hot tea soothes your nerves and calms your emotions. Experiment, and when you find something that helps you, stick with it.

- Remember the role God's Spirit plays in helping you control your emotions. Read about the fruit of the Spirit in Galatians 5:22–23. What fruit is lacking in your life when you let your emotions control you?

16

Envy

Bless your enemies; no cursing under your breath.
Laugh with your happy friends when
they're happy; share tears when they're down.
Get along with each other; don't be stuck-up.
Make friends with nobodies; don't be the great somebody.
Romans 12:15

Read It

As we watch our children grow from sweet, innocent babies into toddlers, it can be shocking to see that one of the first emotions to show itself is envy. Envy is that feeling we get when we see what someone else has—whether that's some superior quality or an achievement, relationship, or possession—and desire it for ourselves (or wish the other person didn't have it either).

Well, now I'm feeling pretty bad about wanting Suzy X's ukulele in fourth grade.

As we watch our children play, it almost seems natural for them to want something that someone else has. But in fact, the desire to obtain a possession that isn't our own is the first sign of envy we witness: there's our precious child eyeing a colorful toy her playmate has . . . and snatching it right out from under her. Tears follow, and we moms rush to intervene: "Sweetie, we don't take things from someone else."

Oh, if only that were the end of our struggle with envy. Wrestling against envy is an ongoing battle. As we get older, perhaps the target of our envy changes from a bright red and yellow rattle to a big house or a husband who washes dishes. Who needs a ukulele anyway?

I love how one friend of mine looks at others who have more than she has. She says that instead of focusing on her lack of that quality or possession, she has learned to turn her focus on the person who has those things and be thankful that they have them. Now, that's putting Romans 12:15 into action! Perhaps, instead of just reminding our children that we don't take things from others, we would do well to add, "and we're happy that they have those things." Then, let's remind ourselves of that too.

Think It

> The truest mark of being born
> with great qualities is being born without envy.
> François de La Rochefoucauld

Live It

- Show your kids how satisfying it can be to banish envy. When someone gets an honor or possession your child envies, help him or her come up with a way to turn the tables on envy and rejoice with the person. Make a personal card of congratulations, invite the person out for ice cream to celebrate, throw a party, or find an article online to share that relates. Even if your kids don't feel happy at first, investing in the other person's joy will help bring them joy as well.

- Celebrate what you have. If you envy your friend's new car, celebrate your old car. Drive through a fast-food restaurant, ice-cream place, or doughnut shop; get a messy treat, then sit in the car and celebrate. After all, your friend can't eat stuff like that in her new car. Find ways to celebrate whatever it is you have.

- Discuss (or read) the fable of the dog and the bone: A dog, carrying a bone, looked into the water and saw a dog who appeared to have a bone bigger than his. Wanting the bigger bone, he tried to take it away from the dog in the river, but it was only his own reflection. In trying to get the "better" bone, he dropped his bone into the river and lost it forever. Challenge your kids to come up with a fable of their own that shows the dangers of envy.

17

Fears

*This resurrection life you received from God is not a timid,
grave-tending life. It's adventurously expectant, greeting
God with a childlike "What's next, Papa?" God's Spirit
touches our spirits and confirms who we really are.
We know who he is, and we know who we are:
Father and children. And we know we are going to
get what's coming to us—an unbelievable inheritance!
We go through exactly what Christ goes through.
If we go through the hard times with him, then we're
certainly going to go through the good times with him!*
Romans 8:15

Read It

I view fear as a necessary evil. I don't like scary movies or
things that jump out at me in the dark, but I respect that
my fear of certain things has kept me from danger many
times in my life. One of my grandchildren seems fearless,
or at least pretty close to it. You may have a child like that.
They're the ones who climb up on the stool and balance
on one leg to get a cookie from the highest shelf in the
kitchen, which you thought was completely out of reach.
They're also the ones most likely to give you gray hair
early. But don't you sometimes admire their boldness?
They just go through life with gusto.

As adults, we don't fear things that go bump in the night like we did as a child; our fears are usually about finances, physical health, or matters relating to our children. And while it's true that fear is an instinct that helps protect us, we need to realize that when our fears become so overwhelming that we can't tackle the tasks we need to progress in life, then we have a problem.

Have you ever seen fear in the eyes of an animal caught in your headlights? The poor thing knows it's in danger, but it just freezes—setting itself up for harm rather than taking steps to get out of the way. We do that too, don't we? When tough times overtake us, sometimes we just freeze—we're paralyzed because we don't know what to do or are afraid to take the necessary steps. We just want to stand still and hope trouble will go around us.

But when we trust and follow God, we have no need to fear. He will give us what we need to face any trouble that comes our way. Romans 8:15 assures us that we are not doomed to a timid life but have received from God a life of power and strength. No, it won't be easy, and you probably will encounter plenty of scary situations. But God will help you to face your fears and overcome them. You'll be able to balance on the firm foundation He gives and reach for the stars.

Think It

*It is our attitude toward events, not events themselves,
which we can control. Nothing is by its own nature
calamitous—even death is terrible only if we fear it.*
Epictetus

Live It

- Does your child have ablutophobia, the fear of washing or bathing; or lachanophobia, a fear of vegetables? Does your boss have allodoxaphobia, the fear of opinions (other than her own)? Does your older sister have cacophobia, the fear of ugliness? Maybe you yourself have ephebiphobia, the fear of teenagers. Fears can sound funny as long as they're not our own—but they're no laughing matter. Identify several of your fears or phobias. Give them a humorous name—Methuselahphobia, fear of aging, or yardstickphobia, fear of not measuring up to confront the fear and reduce its power.

- Face a fear head-on. Make a dental appointment. Agree to speak to your group. Take off your swimsuit cover-up at the pool. Stop plucking those gray hairs. Ask God to give you courage and grace to overcome your fears.

- For every fear that assaults you, meditate on or memorize an appropriate passage of trust and confidence from the Bible. Here are some examples:

Exodus 20:20	Deuteronomy 1:21
Deuteronomy 2:3	Deuteronomy 31:6–8
Psalm 27:3	Psalm 118:6
Psalm 46:1–3	Psalm 56:4
Isaiah 54:4, 14	Isaiah 35:4
Isaiah 41:10	Romans 8:15
Ezekiel 3:9	Joel 2:21
1 John 4:18	2 Timothy 1:7
Hebrews 13:6	

18

Friends

Become wise by walking with the wise;
hang out with fools and watch your life fall to pieces.
Proverbs 13:20

Read It

As moms we worry and even work behind the scenes to ensure that our children have good friends. When I was a camp director, one mother actually offered to pay a child to move away from the bunk next to her child. While that seems a bit over the top, it's perfectly appropriate to be in charge of your children's play dates until they're old enough to make good choices in companions.

But what about *your* "playmates"? Who do you hang around with? Do they build you up or tear you down? Are they helping you to achieve your goals as a Christian wife and mother? Or could it be time to reevaluate your choice of friends?

I once had a friend who complained all the time, and soon I found myself using some of the same phrases she used in my daily conversations. I'm happy to say my life didn't fall to pieces, as the proverb suggests; but I did find myself becoming more and more negative about life. It came to a point where I had to stop, look, and listen: stop and evaluate who my friends were, look around for some other friendships that could help me to be a better person, and listen carefully to my own words to be sure they were glorifying God and not pulling others down.

Just as you are careful who your children associate with, be wise in your own associations as well. Make sure you surround yourself with people who want the best for you, and then you can spur each other on to good works.

Think It

The influence of each human being on others
in this life is a kind of immortality.
John Quincy Adams

Live It

- Look around you. Whose friendships would be beneficial to you? Why? Figure out a way to make contact with one or more of those people this week and start building a friendship.

- Look around again, this time to see who could benefit from what you have to offer as a mentor, example, and friend. Reach out to at least one such person this week and start building a friendship.

- What friends have fallen through the cracks? Renew contact with them this week. Whose friendship was particularly helpful to you at a crucial point in your life? Send a card or pick up the phone and say thanks.

- Nurture the positive friendships you have. Call, get together, share cookies or a joke, go to a movie together, share an article you liked, IM or e-mail these friends. It doesn't take much—just some positive contact now and then.

19

Grace

Let grace, mercy, and peace
be with us in truth and love from
God the Father and from Jesus Christ, Son of the Father!
2 John 1:3

Read It

Think of all the areas of life where grace is needed. That would be pretty much everywhere, wouldn't it? From the new hairstylist who didn't do such a great job on your hair (but didn't mention that it was her first day on the job) to the maddeningly slow cashier at the local grocery store who, perhaps unknown to you, has dyslexia and struggles to memorize the item codes correctly. Or maybe what frustrates you is not having a real-live-person cashier but one of those self-checkout machines where customers have to scan their own items, bag their own merchandise, and then haul their own stuff to the car.

Yes, grace is needed in every area of our lives, every day of our lives. One definition of grace that I love is this: Grace is the enabling power sufficient for progression. Everyday life constantly challenges us, as errors will no doubt be made by others and will affect us. But by forgiving those mistakes that will be made and allowing for correction, we soon see progress. The hairstylist improves, and next time your hair turns out great. The cashier does master those codes and is so speedy and friendly that you choose his lane over anyone else's. The self-checkout . . . well . . . I'm still working on being gracious about those.

God's grace enables us to develop and improve beyond our limitations that include failures, flaws, and mistakes. Without grace, one stumble would stop us from progressing toward our prize—a loving and eternal home with God. But with grace, we have the freedom to explore life, make mistakes, pick ourselves up, and start over. What a gift that is!

Are you teaching your children the value of grace, its meaning and its message? Are you modeling grace in your life, extending it to the neighbors, your children, and your spouse? Your words and example will ultimately teach your children what God's grace does for them. And lastly, are you living your life knowing that God has given you this free gift? I hope you are. God's love for you is "over the top"—He sent His Son to die for you so that you can have power to progress in life and enjoy sweet victory in the end.

While it may take me a while to try a self-checkout again, God, in an instant, forgives me when I get something wrong and gives me another chance. He does the same for you. Will you do it for others?

Think It

The grace of God means something like:
Here is your life. You might never
have been, but you are because the party
wouldn't have been complete without you.
Frederick Buechner

Live It

• Find verses about grace in the Bible. Read them thoughtfully. Meditate on them. Pray that God will give you grace in every situation life throws your way as well as strength to extend His grace to others. Here are some to get you started:

Proverbs 1:8–9	Proverbs 3:34
John 1:16	Romans 3:23–24
2 Corinthians 8:9	2 Corinthians 9:8
Ephesians 1:1–10	Colossians 4:6
1 Timothy 1:12–17	Hebrews 4:14–16
Hebrews 12:15	2 Peter 3:18

• Play or sing songs of grace. Some examples include "God of Grace" by Adam Watts; "Amazing Grace" by Todd Agnew; "Grace" by U2; and "Your Grace Is Enough" by Matt Maher (sung by Chris Tomlin). Play each song multiple times, really focusing on the words and the concept of grace. Perhaps the songs will stick in your head and heart, reminding you of God's grace all day long.

- *Grace* is a word many children don't know. This week, teach your kids grace, not just by your actions, but in words. As you work at extending grace to others or being thankful for God's grace, articulate the word and the concept so your children will learn the term and its fruit in their own lives.

20

Happiness

I'm thanking you, God, from a full heart,
I'm writing the book on your wonders.
I'm whistling, laughing, and jumping for joy;
I'm singing your song, High God.
Psalm 9:1

Read It

Do you have one child who never seems to get the "time to be happy" memo? You know, the one who even on Christmas morning tends to be whiny while opening presents and eating holiday goodies.

Happiness is a broad term for feelings that can range from contentment or general satisfaction to bliss or intense joy. But too often, if we don't feel intense joy all the time, we fool ourselves into thinking we're not happy. We rarely are satisfied to call contentment happiness.

A common pitfall in our modern, prosperous society is to look for happiness in our possessions. Children seem especially prone to this, but many of us adults make the same mistake of equating happiness with how many "toys" we have. The only difference, really, is that grown-up toys are bigger—houses and clothes and cars and jobs. In his letter to the Galatians, the apostle Paul sent us a clear message about "joyless grabs for happiness" and warning that we will not inherit the kingdom of God if we pursue that kind of lifestyle.

Don't get me wrong, God loves for His children to be happy, just like you love to see your children happy. A quick word search brings up more than 250 references to joy in the Bible. But He also wants us to be holy, a word that appears in the Bible more than 650 times. Many times we let our desire to be happy cause us to make poor decisions that are not in keeping with God's will. Ironically, when we do that, we end up unhappy

Perhaps you've gotten to a place in your life where you don't feel happy. It's okay, it happens. We all get confused from time to time and have to hit the reset button and get back into God's desires for us. So how can we find the type of joy described in the Psalm above, the "whistling, laughing, and jumping for joy" joy? That kind of happiness is not based on circumstances but on a deep understanding of God's love for us. And that comes from reading God's Word and asking Him to give you a spirit of contentment in all things. So today spend a little time with your heavenly Father. God loves a happy heart, and He's just waiting to give you one.

Think It

Happiness is not so much in having as sharing. We make a living by what we get, but we make a life by what we give.
Norman MacEwan

Live It

- Every day this week, read one of the following passages. Then pray, asking God to help you be content—happy—in all things.

Job 8:21	Psalm 5:11
Psalm 16:11	Psalm 28:7
Psalm 51:12	Psalm 100
Ecclesiastes 5:19	Matthew 25:21
1 Thessalonians 5:16	1 Timothy 6:6
James 1:2–3	James 5:1

- "Count your blessings, name them one by one," says the old song. Try it. Thank God—aloud—for each blessing. Each is a gift from God, chosen and provided for you by a heavenly Father who loves you.

- Look for ways to laugh every day. Watch a comedy. Make up a joke. Play a wacky, physical game with your kids. Try to walk on your hands. Dress up the dog or cat. See who can make the goofiest face, you or your kids. A little laughter each day reminds the heart that it's happy.

21

Hate

Hatred stirs up dissension, but love covers over all wrongs.
Proverbs 10:12 (NIV)

Read It

Loving someone when hate is by far the easier and more ready emotion is extremely difficult. But of course, *hate* is a strong word . . . or is it? You don't really hate anything or anyone . . . do you? What about that nosy neighbor who comes over just to aggravate you, or the kid down the street who bosses your little one around? Sometimes we gloss it over, but hate might very well be what we're feeling.

The truth is that letting hate have a field day in your head is as dangerous as letting your four-year-old cook supper. Another truth is that as we get older, we're likely to encounter many situations that could stir up this awful emotion. This is true because over time, life, like a pan under a leaky faucet, fills up with more people and events as each year passes. You'll have your share of bosses who challenge you, in-laws who frustrate you, children who aggravate you, and teenagers who irritate you. People make the world go round, but people also can bring out the worst in us. So, what does a person have to do to get along in the world?

The answer is simple; the application is tough. The Bible says that in all we do, love should be our number-one motivation—even when love seems practically impossible to conjure up.

One way to accomplish this is to try to see each person through God's eyes. When you feel negative emotions stirring up, stop, put on your "God glasses," and try to imagine what the offending person looks like from the perspective of your—and that person's—heavenly Father. After all, He looks at us and still loves us. Yep, even when we first wake up, before our first cup of coffee, He loves us. God sees past all of our faults. In return, He asks us, when we see the shortcomings of His other children, to instead of magnifying them with hate, cover them with love.

Think It

*I would permit no man . . . to narrow
and degrade my soul by making me hate him.*
—*Booker T. Washington*

Live It

- When someone stirs up those telltale feelings of (gasp—dare we say it?) hatred, write his or her name on a sticky note or little paper heart and stick it to your mirror or refrigerator. Every time you see it, pray for that person. God can change people—both them and you—and give you unexpected compassion and love.

- This week, make Proverbs 10:12 your rule for living. Don't pass on information that makes someone you dislike look bad. It takes two to quarrel. Don't take the bait and play any role in such conflicts.

- Who in your life is hard to love? Think of at least four good qualities the person has, and try to focus on those.

22

Ignorance

*In a well-furnished kitchen there are not only
crystal goblets and silver platters, but waste cans
and compost buckets—some containers used to serve
fine meals, others to take out the garbage. Become
the kind of container God can use to present any and
every kind of gift to his guests for their blessing.*
2 Timothy 2:20–21

Read It

I was probably eleven or twelve when I first realized the difference between *stupid* and *ignorant*. I don't know why it was such a revelation to me or why I remember it so clearly, but I do. Someone a few years older than I was explained it to us younger kids as we were playing. It was probably prompted by some unkind name-calling. This older friend told us that *stupid* means that someone is not very smart, but *ignorant* simply means that you don't yet know certain information. Up until that point, since I had heard other kids use the words interchangeably to be mean to others, and since we weren't allowed to use either word in our home, I assumed that both were "bad" words.

This new revelation hit right between the eyes. Maybe it made such an impact because I was a skinny, four-eyed preteen who felt pretty stupid about a lot of things.

Suddenly I realized that I wasn't stupid at all—I was just ill informed, and there's a cure for ill informed.

The Bible tells us to study to show ourselves approved, to put on our spiritual armor, to guard our hearts. These are different measures we can take to ensure that we're prepared, not ignorant of how to deal with what life throws at us.

I don't think there's a more desperate feeling than facing some crisis and not being prepared. Remember the school exams you didn't study for? You were ignorant of the knowledge necessary to do well on those tests, and your grades reflected that. But the good news is that you weren't stupid. And you're not now. Yet the tests you face as an adult have bigger consequences than grades. With so much at stake, you can't afford to be unprepared, ignorant of how to succeed.

As a mom, let your children see that you spend time every day preparing for the challenges of life. Communicate with them why you're buying groceries or reading the Bible or studying a parenting book. Your kids need to know that moms and dads do homework too—and that overcoming ignorance is key in improving their quality of life.

Think It

To admit ignorance is to exhibit wisdom.
Ashley Montagu

Live It

- Learn something. Take your kids to the library and select at least one educational book for each family member: a biography of a great person, a how-to book, a lively historical novel, an instructional magazine, or history book. Set aside a couple of times this week to spend together reading your various books and sharing your new knowledge with each other.

- Every day this week, learn a new word together. Challenge family members to try to use each new word in conversation five times that day to cement the word and its meaning in their memories. Choose words at an appropriate level for your children (although you'd be surprised by the high level of words even small children can learn when you make a family game of it). Consider these possibilities:

  - *churlish:* surly; marked by a lack of civility or graciousness
  - *hubris:* exaggerated pride or self-confidence
  - *incontrovertible:* indisputable; not open to question
  - *interpolate:* to insert words into a text or conversation

- *metamorphosis:* a change of physical form, especially by supernatural means; a striking alteration in appearance, character, or circumstances
- *parameters:* limits; boundaries
- *reciprocal:* shared, felt, or shown by both sides
- *usurp:* to seize or take by force or without right (usurp a throne or position of power)
- *vacuous:* empty; lacking content; marked by lack of ideas or intelligence; stupid, inane

- Ask your kids to tell you the most amazing or interesting thing they've learned this year. Let them show off their growing knowledge.

23

Improvements

*I'm not saying that I have this all together,
that I have it made. But I am well on my way,
reaching out for Christ, who has so wondrously
reached out for me. Friends, don't get me wrong:
By no means do I count myself an expert
in all of this, but I've got my eye on the goal,
where God is beckoning us onward—to Jesus.
I'm off and running, and I'm not turning back.*
Philippians 3:12

Read It

When my children were involved in sports, I always loved to see who would get the "Most Improved" award at the end of the season. The most improved athlete, it seemed to me, was the one who was coachable, who would listen and respond to instruction, who was willing to work hard. One year my son won this award. But I have to tell you, he was not happy about it.

His first thought was that he must have been really bad to start with. I explained that even the best ballplayer has room to improve, and in fact, if he doesn't, he won't be very valuable to his team. I also gave my "You must have been ready to listen and eager to learn" congratulatory speech.

Later, as I thought about his reaction, it hit me that most of us are afraid of getting the "Most Improved" award for the same reasons my son expressed. Wouldn't it worry you if you got an award for being the most-improved mom on your street? I'm thinking that's an award that wouldn't go on your fireplace mantel. *Improved—was I that bad?* you'd probably wonder. But think for a minute about the things in life we'd love to see improved: the energy efficiency of our houses, the gas mileage in our cars, or the food in the school cafeteria. In every area of life, we expect and accept improvement, yet we're reluctant to admit needing it ourselves.

I love Paul's admission to the Philippians: "I'm not saying that I have this all together." The truth is, none of us have it all together. We're all works in progress. If we're willing to admit that and to be coached by God, responding to His instruction, we can earn some "Most Improved" awards in life. And that's nothing to be ashamed of.

Think It

The most essential feature of man is his improvableness.
John Fiske

Live It

- Think back five years . . . now ten. What are five areas in which you've grown and improved? How did that improvement happen?

- Now think five . . . ten years down the road. What improvements would you like to have made in your life by then? How can such growth be accomplished? What steps can you take now to start down that path to improvement? Make a plan with measurable goals and milestones. Review it occasionally to help keep yourself on course.

- Set goals for improvement for each of your children. Discuss the goals with them. Talk about ways to achieve those goals, a time frame for achieving them, and a way to celebrate once the goal has been achieved. Encourage and pray for your child as he or she strives to improve in this area.

24

Judging

Don't be nitpickers;
use your head—and heart!—to discern
what is right, to test what is authentically right.
John 7:24

Read It

Once I was called to the principal's office. I can still hear my name being read aloud by my high-school homeroom teacher. I got up from my desk and began the long walk to the office. It's a miracle my brain didn't explode from the quick thinking I was doing as I mentally pored over all of my recent activities, searching for anything that might suggest misconduct and require a visit with the principal. How was I going to defend myself? I didn't even know what I had done wrong.

Some of you have had a similar experience—maybe even had to face a real judge. The job of a court-appointed judge is to determine the guilt or innocence of the accused and then to issue an appropriate sentence. It's an awesome responsibility and not one to be taken lightly.

But on a smaller and more personal scale, we too act as judges, each day making countless small and large assessments. Will we judge rightly and act appropriately?

In John 7:24 I see two bits of wisdom that can help us.

The first is to refrain from nitpicking. If you're constantly looking for the smallest thing to criticize in others, recognize that the nitpicking train has left the station and you're on board. Jump off that train immediately!

The next advice in that verse is to use both your head and your heart when weighing whether something is right or wrong. If we use only our hearts, we'll base our decisions on emotion, not on sound principles. Our emotions are God-given, and they are important; but in judging wisely, they are not always reliable. Your mind also is God-given, and the ability to use your brain and listen to the facts will be your best tool.

Over the years, judging has gotten a bad rap, when in reality we all make judgments hundreds of times a day. Otherwise we couldn't function in life. We do have to judge. But we are called to it in a way that's just and pleasing to God—without criticism, with wisdom, based on facts, and with a healthy measure of grace.

After all, sometimes the principal just wants to know if you'll babysit his kids on Friday night.

Think It

If you get all the facts,
your judgment can be right;
if you don't get all the facts, it can't be right.
Bernard M. Baruch

Live It

- At the grocery store, teach your children how to judge produce, nutritional content of cereal, or the comparative values of different-sized packages of the same product. Explain that "testing" and "discerning" are important and appropriate tasks we must do daily. Discuss the difference between nitpicking people's actions and testing or discerning their character.

- Practice giving people the benefit of the doubt today. Instead of deciding the driver cut you off in traffic to spite you, figure that maybe he just didn't see you. Instead of assuming your new neighbors are the biggest slobs on the block because their trash cans have been at the curb for three days, consider that maybe they're sick or away. Get creative in thinking up innocent explanations for minor annoyances or shortcomings of strangers and acquaintances.

- Set up a family court to settle family disputes. Allow every member to take a turn judging. The only requirement for judges is to follow John 7:24: "Don't be nitpickers; use your head—and heart!— to discern what is right, to test what is authentically right."

25

Kindness

So, chosen by God for this new life of love,
dress in the wardrobe God picked out for you:
compassion, kindness, humility, quiet strength, discipline.
Be even-tempered, content with second place,
quick to forgive an offense.
Colossians 3:12–13

Read It

When was the last time you visited the playground at
your child's school? Having been a school teacher for
twelve years, a camp counselor and director for more
than thirty years, and now a grandmother to ten children,
I've witnessed the wrath children can unleash on one
another more times than I care to remember. It seems
certain personality types just have a hard time at being
nice. I have encountered children who would rather hang
by their toenails and write lines on the chalkboard than
say "I'm sorry."

As a mom, kind behavior is a must-have outfit in
your "wardrobe." Remember that children imitate you,
and just as they play dress-up in grown-ups' clothes, so
they will emulate your words and actions. When I was
teaching, I often wondered where a certain characteristic
of a misbehaving student came from . . . until I met his or

her parents. Kind and caring behavior has to be taught, like everything else, early in life. Communication is a vital part of how we are kind to others—and how we demonstrate that to our kids. But because we're busy, and much of our communication is done by e-mail, cell phone, drive-through windows, and BlackBerries, the opportunities for our kids to see us in kind interaction are fewer than they once were. We have to make a conscious effort to let our children see our kindness in relation to others. We have to live it out loud and on purpose.

Even with your busy schedule, you can involve children in acts of kindness. By simply helping an elderly neighbor, smiling and saying thank you to the attendant at the fast-food window, participating in the Salvation Army drive at Christmas, or speaking kindly to your family, you demonstrate kindness to others. Be sure to reinforce that example by explaining to children why it's important to be kind.

Research shows that children are more likely to comply with adults' wishes when they hear a reasonable and understandable explanation. And what better explanation than that God, who is immeasurably kind to us, wants us to be kind to others to the point that it's as though we are clothed in kindness. Now that's dressing for success!

Think It

> *I expect to pass through life but once.*
> *If, therefore, there be any kindness I can show,*
> *or any good thing I can do to any fellow being,*
> *let me do it now, and not defer or neglect it,*
> *as I shall not pass this way again.*
> William Penn

Live It

- With your children, bake cookies, make handmade seasonal cards, or pick flowers or fresh produce from your garden to share. Let them take the lead in choosing an appropriate project and recipient of your kindness. Let the kids deliver the goodies and a kind word to a neighbor, school or Sunday-school staff, residents of an assisted-living facility, or other group.

- When professionals work in your home or yard, accompany your children as they offer a cold bottle of water or do another small act of kindness.

- Challenge your kids to commit secret, random acts of kindness during the week—to look for opportunities to be kind to someone else. Encourage them to do it not to make a good impression but for the sheer joy of being kind and making someone's day brighter.

26

Language

*Though some tongues just love the taste of gossip,
those who follow Jesus have better uses for
language than that. Don't talk dirty or silly. That kind
of talk doesn't fit our style. Thanksgiving is our dialect.*
Ephesians 5:4

Read It

I don't know about you, but I cannot speak any language
but English. Oh, I took two years of Spanish in school,
but basically, I'm no further ahead than a three-year-
old who watches *Dora the Explorer*. However, I value the
language I do know and don't take for granted the ability
to communicate my thoughts, emotions, and needs with
those around me. That's what language does—it connects
us to others.

A great day for any mom and dad is when their baby
says "Da-Da" or "Ma-Ma" for the first time. Parents even
argue good-naturedly about which was said first, each
claiming the victory and thus the closest connection with
their child. Neither parent realizes or cares that a few
years from that triumphant moment, he or she will think
something like, *Please don't say "Daddy" ["Mommy"] one more
time!*

Language is interesting, isn't it? Who hasn't wondered
at the origins of words. Why is a tree called a tree? Who

makes up all these words? Sometimes I wonder if we spend more time wondering about the origin of a particular word than about the impact our words have on others. Remember your mother's admonition "If you can't say anything nice, don't say anything at all"? It sounds a lot like the advice the apostle Paul gave the Ephesians. Except that Paul—God, really, speaking through Paul—doesn't want us to settle for not saying anything at all; he wants us to put our words to better service.

We have better uses for our language than to gossip and talk silly. Mark Twain once said, "I can live for two months on a good compliment." He understood the power of positive words. But remember that words leave our mouths like toothpaste out of a tube: once spoken, they cannot be put back in. So use good judgment before sending your words out into the world. Ask yourself, as a friend of mine once asked her grandchild, "Are these words better left inside my head or out there for the world to use?" Then you'll be able to speak with confidence—and without regret.

Think It

Kind words can be short and easy to speak,
but their echoes are truly endless.
Mother Teresa

Live It

- Make a family words chart. Write each person's name at the far-left side of the page. Put a star or sticker beside the person's name each time someone hears that person saying something encouraging, kind, or affirming.

- Give each family member at least one compliment every day this week. If you're not spontaneous or think you might forget, write them all down. Make them thoughtful, meaningful, and individualized for the specific strengths and gifts of each child. Then consider packing one in with your child's lunch, placing it on her pillow, hiding it in his backpack, or finding some other creative way to share these uplifting words.

- If you're trying to break your children—or yourself—of the habit of using certain words, try this: when anyone else catches the person saying the undesirable words, he should make a sound like a foul buzzer (or lightly flick the person's arm with a finger). Such an activity is fun for kids to play and makes everyone more conscious of their words. And you just might break some bad habits.

27

Listening

Post this at all the intersections, dear friends:
Lead with your ears, follow up with your tongue,
and let anger straggle along in the rear.
James 1:19

Read It

Don't you love the image that this verse paints? You drive
up to an intersection as you're lecturing your teenager
over a behavior you're not happy with and BAM! A huge
sign appears right before you that reads, "Lead with your
ears!"

But you're too far into the lecture to stop and you proceed to finish it off. Then another intersection and another
sign. This time you take note. You stop talking and decide
to just listen. Your child is in shock, but you're determined
to wait patiently to hear what's going on in his life.

Listening, like letter writing, is a dying form of
communication. Many young parents allow or even
encourage their children to express themselves whenever
and wherever they please. Adults do the same. As a society,
we're quick to complain, whether we're in our car yelling
at another driver who cut us off or on the phone with the
cable repair service. It seems everyone is screaming, and
too few people bother to listen.

The term *tuned-out* became popular in the 1960s—young people were accused of tuning out the establishment; young people said it was the establishment that had tuned them out. It's the old "Which came first, the chicken or the egg?" scenario. But the truth is, assigning guilt never solves a problem.

We all need to heed the advice James gave the Christians of his day and learn to lead with our ears. It's a form of pride to want to have the last word in a conversation. And pride has no place in your business life, your home life, or your church life. Learn to listen to others before sharing your thoughts. Set your tuning dial to husband, children, and others. You'll be surprised what you'll learn—and how much better your relationships can be—when you do.

Think It

I think the one lesson I have learned
is that there is no substitute for paying attention.
Diane Sawyer

Live It

- Go for a ride with your son or daughter, just the two of you. With the passing miles, you'll leave behind the regular inhibitions and be able to converse freely. Make it a point to truly listen. You might be surprised to learn what your child really thinks about things.

- Practice active listening. Here are the basics:

    1. Don't interrupt when someone else is speaking.

    2. Resist the urge to think about what you're going to say in response, and truly listen to what is being said.

    3. Summarize aloud what you heard the person say and ask if you heard correctly before responding with what you want to say.

    4. Don't get defensive or accusatory.

- Post a homemade warning sign in your house in the shape of a road sign to remind you: LISTEN!

28

Men

God spoke: "Let us make human beings in our image,
make them reflecting our nature."
Genesis 1:26

Read It

You will find that gaining an understanding of anything in life brings about a better acceptance of that
thing. Think about any time you're introduced to new
technology, whether it's an iPhone, an MP3 player, or
a fancy new digital camera. You likely feel a bit intimi-
dated by it, even confused, until you read the instructions and study it. As you gain an understanding of its
characteristics and achieve the knowledge needed to
get the benefits you want, you become more accepting
and more comfortable with it.

While I hate to compare men to another piece of
technology, the analogy does work. We women need
to take the time to understand men better. Moms,
your relationships with the men in your life will have a
tremendous impact on your children, both your girls and
your boys.

I am troubled by the amount of "man-cutting" I see
on television and in the movies: characterizations that
diminish the role of men and make them appear stupid or

otherwise incapable. Sure, we all see the humor in scenes where the dad can't put up Christmas lights without falling off the roof, or the husband bungles the job of diapering the baby. I admit, I have laughed at them myself. But our impressionable children are being bombarded with these images, and their views of what makes a man a real man are being shaped by Hollywood. Classic television shows that presented a healthy family, like *Father Knows Best*, are being laughed at today—but more for seeming out of date than for being humorous.

Children need to understand that men and women are different, but different doesn't mean stupid or incapable. Focusing on the good traits of the men in your life will not only send a positive message to your children but also will make your man feel special, loved, and needed. Point out to your children the good things about these men, and they'll begin to understand that God made us different for a reason. It takes all kinds to make a world, so seek to understand, value, and embrace those wonderful differences!

Think It

*Treat people as if they were what they ought to be
and you help them become what they
are capable of becoming.*
Johann Wolfgang von Goethe

Live It

- Make it a point to let your children hear you expressing your respect, love, and appreciation for the men in your life, especially your husband. Encourage your children to express their respect and love as well.

- Ask your husband to tell you one thing he wishes you knew or better understood or appreciated about him. Really listen—don't laugh or get defensive— and then try to see things from his perspective.

- Do something with or for your husband that you know he would love but that you normally don't do because you don't like it. Maybe it's going fishing or to a ball game or watching wrestling or a "guy" blow-'em-up movie with no plot and lousy acting. Try to observe what it is he likes about the pastime—and don't act like you're doing him a favor. Do let him know that you're trying to please and honor him—just for being himself.

29

Mistakes

*Consider it a sheer gift, friends, when tests
and challenges come at you from all sides.
You know that under pressure, your faith-life is
forced into the open and shows its true colors.
So don't try to get out of anything prematurely.
Let it do its work so you become mature and
well-developed, not deficient in any way.*

James 1:2–3

Read It

When was the last time you made a mistake? Chances are it was today. Mistakes are a part of our daily life, and they come in all shapes and sizes—from adding too much salt to the soup to forgetting to shut the car door. And the results are just as varied. Too much salt just means the soup tastes bad; but an open car door could result in a dead battery or worse—severe damage to your car and a costly repair bill. Some mistakes can even be deadly, like taking or giving a wrong medication.

But a mistake, by definition, is not a sin. It's the result of misjudgment, carelessness, or forgetfulness. I remember the time my four-year-old thought laundry detergent would make a lawn mower work. His misjudgment caused a very unhappy grandpa to have to repair his mower. And I'll never forget the time my carelessness led me to leave the sunroof open on my husband's car, and a rainstorm blew in.

For some reason we think that as we age and mature, the number of mistakes we make will diminish. But really, we just make different mistakes. We will never be exempt from error. There isn't a "no more mistakes" card we get when we pass eighteen or twenty-one or sixty-five. What we do get with maturity is a better understanding of what constitutes a mistake—and we learn how to accept the mistakes in our lives and to patiently deal with the mistakes of others.

At least, that's the plan. Moms, you will continue to make mistakes as you parent your children. While I am a firm believer in parenting with confidence—the old "never let them see you sweat" principle—there will be times when it's in the best interest of your children to see you admit to a mistake, especially as they get older and are more mature themselves. It's also important for your children to observe a mom who is patient and forgiving toward others who make mistakes. Confess to your kids when you've made a mistake—and when they make one, be willing to extend a little grace. After all, isn't that exactly what our heavenly Father does for us?

Think It

To make no mistakes is not in the power of man;
but from their errors and mistakes the wise
and good learn wisdom for the future.
Plutarch

Live It

- On a piece of paper, list some mistakes you've made in your life. Then feed the paper through the shredder to represent the forgiveness you've received through Christ. Now write down some of the mistakes those around you have made that have hurt or frustrated you. What will you do with this sheet of paper and the transgressions it represents?

- When you make a mistake, admit it quickly. Ask your child (or whoever is the offended person) to forgive you. Remember, not doing so is another mistake.

- Start a mistake jar. Use a container that is chipped, bent, broken, or marred in some way, and label it "~~Misstakes~~ ~~Messtakes~~ ~~Misteaks~~ Mistakes." When someone in the family makes a mistake, he or she should make a monetary contribution to the jar (the amount should depend on the net worth of the mistake maker and the impact of the mistake). When enough money has been collected, spend it on a special treat for the family. Use this as an illustration of the cost of mistakes, as well as the truth that with a teachable, humble attitude and the Lord's help, something good can also come from our mistakes.

30

No

*It's in Christ that we find out
who we are and what we are living for.
Long before we first heard of Christ
and got our hopes up, he had his eye on us,
had designs on us for glorious living, part
of the overall purpose he is working out
in everything and everyone.*
Ephesians 1:11–12

Read It

The word *no* is hardly one you expect to see featured in a devotional book. This simple two-letter word is often as absent in today's parenting toolbox as cloth diapers. Yet it is a vital tool for building strong children with the coping skills needed to tackle life's many distractions.

Too often I've observed parents tell their kids "No!" three or four times . . . and then give in just to stop the whining and complaining. Strangely, I don't remember my mother doing that. Once she said no, the more you asked, the more likely it became that you would *never* get what you were begging for.

What has changed in our society to cause us to have such a difficult time with the word *no*? Perhaps part of the problem is that as we've become more affluent, the yeses in life far outweigh the nos. Many families can afford almost anything their children ask for. And "for everything else, there's MasterCard." At least that's what the advertisements tell us. Basically, we don't have to say no to anything . . . we can just charge it.

What we can't charge is character, honesty, persever-ance, accountability, self-respect, and responsibility. But a timely, well-chosen "No" can help develop those things in your children. Parents saying no helps kids learn to manage their wants and desires and to understand that "having it all" isn't the most important thing in life. It also gives them a living example of God's love and desires for us; while God loves us and wants us to be all we can be, He knows that in order for that to happen, His answer to some of our requests must be no. In His infinite wisdom, He knows what is best for us.

And although we moms aren't all-knowing, we're pretty good at knowing what's best for our kids. We just need the courage to stick to our convictions. In those times when you're about to say yes when you should say no, listen to that "mom-intuition" that's telling you to hang tough. Childhood is short; but instead of using that as an excuse to indulge, look at it as a limited opportunity to teach godly principles to your children that will endure and serve them well in their lives as adults.

Think It

In the final analysis it is not what you do
for your children but what you have taught
them to do for themselves that will make
them successful human beings.
Ann Landers

Live It

- Look in a mirror. Practice saying no. See what it looks and feels like. Say it again. Repeat it ten times or more. Now, when you need to say it to your kids, say it . . . say it again . . . and stick to it.

- Think back to when you were a kid. What was one time your parents said no to something you really wanted, and in hindsight, you understand how much better for you it was that they did? When you're tempted to give in to your kids when you really should say no, remember that story and take courage.

- How seriously do your kids take you? When you say no, do they believe you mean no, or do they believe you're really saying maybe or "push harder"? What must you do to get them to properly respect you when you say no?

Nutrition

31

*Learn to appreciate and give
dignity to your body, not abusing it, as is so
common among those who know nothing of God.*
1 Thessalonians 4:4–5

Read It

Monday, spaghetti; Tuesday, chicken; Wednesday, McDonald's; the seemingly never-ending job of providing food for your family can be overwhelming. I remember that first trip to the grocery store to stock my cabinets as a newlywed. It was fun picking out the food that would complete our first week's menu. Now, after thousands of meals and more burned rolls than I can count, going to the grocery store is about as fun as holding a wiggly toddler with a sticky sucker.

Yet on a recent mission trip, I was reminded how blessed we are. In that foreign country we were served beans and rice meal after meal after meal . . . but I never saw a child turn up her nose at the food she was given. There was no whining or complaining, and no one asked for something other than what was being served. It was a scene rarely duplicated in America, where most people have plenty and great variety, and it was a wonderful lesson in thankfulness for having what is necessary.

We live in a nation where necessity doesn't drive our food choices—our desires do. We ask our children what they want for dinner, forgetting the implied assumption that we can provide all they could possibly need.

Most of us don't want to change where we live, nor should we; but we can change our relationship with food. As moms in this blessed society, our challenge is not finding enough food to feed our family but finding the right kinds of foods and giving our children the tools they need to make wise food choices. I realize that many of you, like me, are "cooking challenged." A magnet on my refrigerator reads, "I only have a kitchen because it came with the house." But it is because we are so blessed as a nation that I can even joke about the goings-on in my kitchen. I am incredibly grateful for the plenty my family enjoys, but I still have a responsibility to teach my children that a healthy diet is vital to helping them grow, develop, and do well in school.

Good nutrition is necessary to prevent disease, and it allows both adults and children to function productively. People eat for many reasons, but the only reason that counts is our health. If you're struggling with providing proper nutrition for yourself and your family, now is the time to get a handle on it. Start slowly, by finding some healthful recipes and making smarter choices at fast-food restaurants. If you need more help, purchase a book, look online, or visit a health club. Start today to make a difference in the lives of your children that will last a lifetime. Remember, your body is on loan from God; take care of it!

Think It

Protect your health.
Without it you face a serious
handicap for success and happiness.
Harry F. Banks

Live It

- Discuss the components of a healthy diet as presented in the nutritional food pyramid: grains (breads), vegetables, fruits, oils, milk (dairy), and meat and beans (protein). Visit www.mypyramid .gov for more information. Keeping these food groups in mind and striving for balance, allow each child to plan one well-balanced, nutritious meal for your family this week. You may also want to go through the recipes and help each child make up a shopping list. Then shop together for the items you'll need.

- Try one new vegetable, fruit, or other healthful food each week with your family. Make it a fun adventure.

- Next time you're with your kids at their favorite fast-food restaurant, get a copy of the nutritional information. Go over it together and determine which foods are the best choices nutritionally and calorie-wise. Encourage your kids to be aware of the nutritional content of the food they eat and be able to interpret labels wisely to get the best product for their money.

32

Opportunities

Dear, dear Corinthians, I can't tell you how much I
long for you to enter this wide-open, spacious life. We didn't
fence you in. The smallness you feel comes from within you.
Your lives aren't small, but you're living them in a small way.
I'm speaking as plainly as I can and with great affection.
Open up your lives. Live openly and expansively!
2 Corinthians 6:11–12

Read It

Don't you love the confident spirit of a child who wants
to be an astronaut or president of the United States? If
you haven't done it in a while, sit down with your children
and let them share their dreams for the future with you.
It's refreshing to hear how open they are to whatever
comes their way.

We've all heard the expression that opportunity knocks;
we just have to open the door. And we believe it . . . well,
we sort of believe it. Perhaps you feel like the only knocks
on your door are from bill collectors or the neighbors'
kids looking for a snack. But in reality, opportunity does
knock every day; it's just that sometimes the noise of our
lives gets too loud for us to hear the knock.

Maybe you feel too busy to take on anything else, and
at times in your life that might be true. But God wants you
to stay open and alert to opportunities to grow as a wife,

mom, friend, worker, or all of the above. Opportunities are possibilities that something could happen due to favorable conditions surrounding that thing. Children believe the conditions are always favorable for them to do whatever they dream to do. I have one of those home karaoke machines, and every one of my grandchildren thinks he or she has an opportunity to be on *American Idol*. And guess what—they do! The opportunity is there, even if the likelihood of it happening may not be great.

Maturity is what helps us adults discern which opportunities we should pursue, but it's also something we sometimes hide behind in order to avoid opening a new door. And believe me, God has some great opportunities behind those doors. Here are three things to consider as you look for opportunities: First, you must have desire. Next, have in mind some general idea of what you're looking for or a direction you're wanting to go in. And finally, use your gift of discernment to decide which particular opportunity offers the right path for you to take.

Once those elements are in place, the next time you hear a knock, answer confidently and see what's behind that door!

Think It

When one door closes, another door opens;
but we often look so long and so regretfully upon the
closed door that we do not see the ones which open for us.
Alexander Graham Bell

Live It

- With each child, sit down and outline the opportunities they have right now. These can include school opportunities, chances to play a sport or an instrument, opportunities to go to church, join a club, etc. You and your child may be surprised by the sheer number and variety of opportunities available. Discuss which options are most beneficial or appealing, and map out a plan for maximizing your opportunities.

- Now do the same for yourself. What opportunities should you be pursuing right now? How will you do that?

- In everything you do today, try to see it as an opportunity. Even when it's something you'd rather not do, an opportunity is waiting. Your challenge is to figure out what it is. For instance, being stuck in traffic might be an opportunity to pray or to learn patience. Getting bad news might be an opportunity to display grace and trust in God. Now you try it.

33

Overwhelmed

*God can do anything, you know—far more than you could
ever imagine or guess or request in your wildest dreams!
He does it not by pushing us around but by working
within us, his Spirit deeply and gently within us.*
Ephesians 3:20–21

Read It

In the dictionary, the word *mom* should be right
next to the word *overwhelmed*. I am convinced there's
not a group of people who feel more consistently
overwhelmed than moms do, especially mothers of
young children. The constant calling of your name,
that crazy need your children have to eat every day,
the barrage of papers from school you have to weed
through every night. And if you're a single mom, your
responsibilities are multiplied! Yep, it's just a wee bit
overwhelming.

Since my children are older now, I know you expect me
to say "Enjoy the moment" or "They grow up so fast" or
"This time will pass." Blah, blah, blah. Not to disappoint
you—I am going to say all of those things, because they're
true. But I'm also going to warn you that even as your
children get older, even after they leave home, you will
still feel overwhelmed.

Encouraging, right? Just what you wanted to hear! But it's true. You will be the mom in your family for as long as you live. And while the joys of being a grandmother are indescribable, trust me: you will have overwhelming days in that role too.

God never promised that any job He entrusts to us will be easy or stress-free. What He promises is that He will walk beside us and lighten our load if we let Him. Acknowledging and believing that will help you to breathe more deeply and appreciate whatever stage of life you're in. Beyond that, here are some suggestions for those days when running away from home sounds like a perfectly good plan.

1. Know that you are justified in feeling overwhelmed—being a mom is a tough job!

2. Ask a neighbor, church friend, or family member to trade kids with you for a few hours a week. Schedule the time on a regular basis so you can look forward to it each week.

3. Find a local fitness club that offers child care. Even if you don't work out, pretend you are just to get the break.

4. Find a hobby that you enjoy and feel passionate about.

5. Adopt a 1950s-mom trait and send the kids outside or to their rooms to play for thirty minutes. This will not kill them.

6. Lastly, don't blame others for your not being happy. Feeling overwhelmed usually means you aren't taking enough time for yourself. But it's no one's responsibility but your own to figure this out. Please keep in mind that neither your friend nor your mom, your mother-in-law, not even your husband, can read your mind to know you need help. An honest look at what is happening in your life will either help you discover that you really have more time than you think, or help you find ways to make a little more time for you. Beware that some overwhelmedness is self-imposed—don't defeat yourself.

One more thing: take comfort in knowing that God cannot wear out. No matter how busy you are, He can keep up.

Think It

*The shortest way to do many things
is to do only one at a time.
Richard Cecil*

Live It

- Read Psalm 61:1–4. Write your own psalm or prayer crying out to God, telling Him how overwhelmed you feel and how much you need His help.

- Don't let pride get in your way. You're not Superwoman. No one really expects you to have it all together. Don't be afraid to let someone know you feel overwhelmed and need help, no matter what part of your life is overwhelming you. If you don't have a support system, many churches are willing to help. And don't overlook community programs. Today, before you're overwhelmed, develop a list of helpers and resources you can turn to for help when you most need it.

- Many churches offer monthly parents' night (or day) out when moms can leave their children in safe hands and get some time away. Look for this in your area. Or ask your church if they'd consider starting one.

34

Past

Where is the god who can compare with you—wiping the slate clean of guilt, turning a blind eye, a deaf ear, to the past sins of your purged and precious people? You don't nurse your anger and don't stay angry long, for mercy is your specialty. That's what you love most. And compassion is on its way to us. You'll stamp out our wrongdoing. You'll sink our sins to the bottom of the ocean. You'll stay true to your word to Father Jacob and continue the compassion you showed Grandfather Abraham—everything you promised our ancestors from a long time ago.
Micah 7:18–20

Read It

I love history. I love seeing how events in the past bring us to the present and plant the seeds for the future. I love knowing that my grandmother's parents came to Oklahoma on the Trail of Tears and that my great-grandfather owned land as an Indian. Being connected to my past brings me feelings of hope and security. I cherish the times I sat with my grandmother as she shared these stories with me.

Another memorable illustration of the past connecting to the present is in the movie *The Lion King*. If you are a mom of small children, you've probably seen it so many times you can quote it. Remember the ending? Simba and Nala, only lion cubs at the beginning of the movie, are grown and hold up their new baby while the song "Circle of Life" is sung. The camera takes a panoramic view of the land they now rule over, and it's all you can do to not cry like a baby. That dramatic scene represents Simba and Nala passing on to a new generation the lessons they had learned and the life they had built.

The Old Testament is full of stories telling us about God's people and how they were to pass down from generation to generation the stories of their heritage and faith. Sadly, sometimes we look at our past as more of a book to be locked away than a chapter to be included in our life story

Not everything in my past brings me feelings of hope and security. Some things bring me pain and sadness. But they're still part of who I am. Your life story is the same way. Some things about your past may be embarrassing or make your heart ache, but others will bring you peace and happiness. Those are the things you have to learn to focus on.

Holding on to the negative part of your past only means you're giving those events power over you. Learn to recognize when this is happening, and take control. The Bible tells us to press on, forgetting what is behind and keeping our eyes on the goal of having a home in heaven. Just as Simba and Nala had to endure many hardships before their circle of life was complete, you will as well.

But at the end of your story, God will hold you up with pride, and there won't be a dry eye in the house.

Think It

It is foolish to try to live on past experience. It is very dangerous, if not a fatal habit, to judge ourselves to be safe because of something that we felt or did twenty years ago.
Charles H. Spurgeon

Live It

- Write down your life story. Share it with your children.

- As a family, work on re-creating your family tree and family history through pictures, mementos, and stories. Even if you can't go back very far, capture what you do know and the current events of your life. When your children are grandparents, this will be history long past—but now never forgotten.

- Make a family-history quilt using pieces of cloth that represent individual family members and special events (baby's old blanket, Grandma's special blue dress, etc.). With a fabric pen (or stitching with thread if you're ambitious) write your family tree on the squares with family names; birth, marriage, and death dates; and other important information.

Peace

35

*Run away from infantile indulgence. Run after
mature righteousness—faith, love, peace—joining
those who are in honest and serious prayer before God.
Refuse to get involved in inane discussions;
they always end up in fights. God's servant must not be
argumentative, but a gentle listener and a teacher
who keeps cool, working firmly but patiently with
those who refuse to obey. You never know how or
when God might sober them up with a change of heart
and a turning to the truth, enabling them to escape the
Devil's trap, where they are caught and held captive,
forced to run his errands.*
2 Timothy 2:22–26

Read It

I was a teenager in the late 1960s and early '70s. Yes, that means I had long, straight hair and the ability to make a peace sign on command. *Peace* was probably the most widely used word on posters for those in my generation. We were so confident that we had the answers to a world full of problems—all we had to do, as the famous song says, was "give peace a chance." As it turns out, we were willing to give it a chance; we just didn't realize how hard it would be.

A quick look at two three-year-olds playing gives us a reminder of the difficulty as they fight over a toy that's already half-broken. Peace wears an expensive price tag—someone has to be willing to either give up or at least partially give in to another's wishes or actions. And there's the rub.

Sadly, wars are fought, parents are divorced, siblings refuse to speak to each other, and friends decide to separate—all because the parties involved will not give in to each other. It is our human nature to want to hold on to what we believe is rightly ours. But the Bible teaches us a different way. Before the Beatles sang a note about peace, before holding up two fingers in a V signified anything but that you wanted two of something, and before people rallied and marched against war, God was crying out for His children to give peace a chance!

As moms we are called to keep an atmosphere of peace in our home. Wow! That's pretty heavy, dude (as we said in the '70s). I agree, it is; but it's true. Your children depend on you for so many things—food, clean clothes, shelter—but they also depend on you to establish an atmosphere of God-honoring peace and stability in your home. That's not to say there won't be disagreements, even arguments in your home; it just means that you need to apply the principles God gave us in Scripture to resolve them.

Creating an atmosphere that is mostly—notice, I did say *mostly*—calm and respectful will give your children the best opportunity to grow and develop in all areas of their lives. Life is hard enough for kids these days; give them a home that is a place of rest for them, not another war zone.

Think It

He is the happiest,
be he king or peasant,
who finds peace in his home.
Johann Wolfgang von Goethe

Live It

- No matter how large or small the conflicts in your home, your family just might benefit from a timely "peace council." Set aside an hour to work through things. Allow all parties in any dispute to present their side. All members must agree to keep calm and not let emotions run high or use accusatory or harsh language. Ask each person involved in any conflict to suggest possible solutions and compromises, while those not personally involved can mediate and bring a new perspective.

- Much of the peace in your home starts with you, as the mother. Step back. Lighten up. Ask God to give you peace and to spread peace in your family through you.

- On a portable chalkboard or dry-erase board, make a peace sign to hang in a prominent place in your home. The sign should read, "_____ days of peace" (fill in the blank with the number of days your family has gone without conflict). When World War III breaks out, the sign goes back to zero. See how long a streak your family can keep up—with God's help.

36

Personality

Know this: GOD is God, and God, GOD.
He made us; we didn't make him.
We're his people, his well-tended sheep.
Psalm 100:3

Read It

When my three children were little and played the "That's not fair!" card, I always replied that God wasn't fair to me because He gave me three very different personalities to deal with. Not only do we encounter our children's unique (and sometimes conflicting) personalities daily, but we also deal with our husband's, our coworker's, our sibling's, and on and on. We assess and adjust to personalities all day long until sometimes we're exhausted at the effort. We begin to feel like an old car with a stick shift that can't seem to find the right gear for a smooth ride. One child enters the room and you change gears. Your response to that child makes another cry and you shift gears again. Your husband walks in and you're not willing to shift again, so the ride gets bumpy.

Guess what? Your mom went through the same thing. As an adult, you can now see how different you and your siblings are.

Personality is made up of patterns of thoughts, feelings, and behaviors—characteristics that make a person unique—and these traits tend to remain consistent throughout a lifetime. Think about your siblings again. Have their personalities changed over the years? I can hear some of you crying right now—"You mean my child will never change!" But there is some good news here: people can learn to behave in a better way even though their natural tendency is to stay the same.

While you may not understand everyone's personality, you can understand this: God made each of us uniquely different for a purpose. You can embrace the different personalities and seek to learn what will help each person in your life grow closer to God. You can stop worrying about treating your children the same and begin treating each one as he or she needs to be treated. It does take more of an effort, but your little ones are worth it—and in the end, you will be blessed.

Think It

Men have yet to learn the value of human personality.
The fact that a person is white, or black, or yellow,
of one race or another, of one religion
or that—these things are not all-important.
It is the human personality that should come first.
John R. Van Sickle

Live It

- Pick up a book about personality types at the library or bookstore. Look for insights in identifying the different personalities in your household and how they can get along better. Such books can be helpful in showing you how best to respond to the unique needs of each of your children.

- Is your daughter sweet like sugar? Your teenager hot like a jalapeño pepper? Think up a food, spice, or cooking ingredient that symbolizes the personality of each member of your family. When personality differences exasperate you, try to think of these differences as important diverse flavors that make your family more interesting and stronger.

- Is your son's personality just like your dad's? Does your daughter's temperament remind you of your sister? Talk to them (or any relative or friend whose personality is like one of your kids'). Let them help you understand what motivates, frustrates, and defines them and how you can best deal with them.

37

Pride

Pride lands you flat on your face;
humility prepares you for honors.
Proverbs 29:23

Read It

Have you ever noticed that the middle letter in the word *pride* is *I*? What a great reminder to all of us that if our focus is on ourselves, we might have a pride problem. Pride is a preoccupation with self, and it usually leads us to think more highly of ourselves than we should—to think we are better or more deserving than others.

I'm convinced pride was a huge factor in Eve's decision to eat the forbidden fruit in the Garden of Eden. When the serpent told Eve that her eyes would be opened and she would be like God, it was all over: she let her pride, her desire to be on top of everything, to know more, get in the way of making a wise decision. And she landed flat on her face, so to speak.

Of course, there's also the kind of pride we can have in things like our family heritage or our college football team. But that's not the pride we're talking about today. The kind of destructive pride we're talking about gave Eve the feeling that she deserved the knowledge that eating the fruit would give her, and she took it on herself to get it. Like all sin, the root of the pride problem is a heart issue—it's not about the action so much as it is about the heart of the one who is taking the action. First Eve's heart rebelled against God, and then she directly disobeyed Him with her actions.

Pride like that isn't reserved for Bible stories. It can rear its ugly head in even the most everyday experiences if we're not careful. If you're driving your children to every after-school activity available simply because you love them and want to challenge them to grow, that's great. If you're doing it because you're secretly in a race for "Mom of the Year" award, that's pride. If you entertain others in your home because God wants you to be hospitable, that's good. But if you're doing it so that others will think more highly of you, that's pride. While the activities might be the same, the attitude of the heart may be very different—and that's what counts with God.

God doesn't give out trophies, but He does give blessing and honor to those who humble themselves, submit to His guidance, and depend on His strength.

Think It

A man given to pride
is usually proud of the wrong thing.
Henry Ford

Live It

- Read Proverbs 16:18—"Pride goes before destruction, a haughty spirit before a fall" (NIV). If your children are young, read Dr. Seuss's *Yertle the Turtle*. Discuss the consequences of pride.

- Identify a handful of things—accomplishments, gifts, possessions—that make you proud. Prayerfully examine your heart. Do you feel proper self-respect, full of gratitude to God, or do you feel superior to others and want them to see and acknowledge your goodness? If so, ask God to forgive you and change your heart.

- Challenge each family member to memorize Proverbs 16:18. When anyone suspects another family member of having this destructive kind of pride, he or she should say "Proverbs 16:18!" as a warning.

38

Quality Time

*We pray that you'll live well for the Master, making him
proud of you as you work hard in his orchard. As you learn
more and more how God works, you will learn how to do
your work. We pray that you'll have the strength to stick it
out over the long haul—not the grim strength of gritting
your teeth but the glory-strength God gives. It is strength
that endures the unendurable and spills over into joy,
thanking the Father who makes us strong enough to take
part in everything bright and beautiful that he has for us.*

Colossians 1:10–12

Read It

The age-old discussion of whether spending quality
time with our children is more important than spending
quantity time with them has been around since women
decided to be more visible in the workforce and felt the
need to defend their decision. Working moms argue that
it's the quality of the time we spend with our children
that matters, while stay-at-home proponents argue that
there's no substitute for the amount of time a child needs
to be around a parent. I'm not going to say that one is
more important than the other, because I believe they're
both essential to the well-being and development of our
children. Several studies suggest that children who are

involved with their families, both in the amount of time and the type of activities, are less prone to violence, drug and alcohol abuse, and self-respect issues than children who lead lives more separate from their parents.

God gave us all the same twenty-four hours in every day. Try as we might, we cannot squeeze any more time out of our days. We have been given a set quantity of time. We should, however, try to get the most for our money, so to speak. God asks us to live well for Him and to make Him proud by using those twenty-four hours we've been given to bring Him glory. That's quality of life.

It seems almost cliché in a book for moms to state the obvious: that the most important gift you can give your child is your love, time, and attention. But I couldn't write a mom book and leave that out! Does giving your child that gift mean that you must devote all of your free time to your children as a way of compensating for the time you spend away from them? Of course not. For the most part, children feel more loved and secure when rules and routines stay in place. Quality time doesn't necessarily need an agenda; it's more a way of life. Here are some ways to accomplish this—if you're not already doing these things, give them a try.

1. Eat together every day—don't worry, eating at a restaurant counts. More important, use mealtimes to communicate. Play a simple game of "good

thing/bad thing," letting each child tell something good and bad about his or her day.

2. Get involved in your children's after-school activities. This can be as simple as asking to see their homework or attending their practices just to cheer them on.

3. Plan a family vacation, even if you have a limited budget. Kids love camping out or taking a trip to the local zoo.

4. Play their games from time to time. Learn about their favorite video game, or start a puzzle together.

5. Use valuable commute time to talk about upcoming events or past events. Ask lots of questions. And listen!

6. Read together, and discuss what you read.

The list of options is virtually endless, but the goal is the same—put your family high on your priority list. The payoff will be worth it!

Think It

Not merely what we do,
but what we try to do and why,
are the true interpreters of what we are.
C. H. Woodward

Live It

- An old children's song said that the way to spell *JOY* is "Jesus, Others, and You." It reminded kids that when you put Jesus and others ahead of yourself, you'd spell joy in your life. This week, be sure to follow the advice of that song. Devote some quality time to each of these in their proper order—Jesus, Others (in this case, your family), and You.

- Let one child each week choose a special quality-time activity to do as a family or just with you.

- Are you spending more quality time with your kids or with your computer/television/hobby/shopping mall/charity work/job/_____ (fill in the blank)? For one week, take a break from whatever consumes much of your best time. Instead, devote that time to what's truly important—your family.

39

Reality

*Dear friends, carefully build yourselves up in this most
holy faith by praying in the Holy Spirit, staying right
at the center of God's love, keeping your arms open
and outstretched, ready for the mercy of our Master,
Jesus Christ. This is the unending life, the real life!*

Jude 1:20–21

Read It

Sometimes I feel like I'm in some strange movie where no
one can believe anything they read or hear. Wait! That is
where I live! That's where we all live.

Beside the fact that reality TV has taken "reality" to a
new level, we are constantly told "facts" from news reports
that change as quickly as we can change the channels; we
watch infomercials making claims about products when
only yesterday we read a report stating how false those
claims are; and we read those magazines (only while we're
waiting in line at the grocery store, of course) containing
every bizarre story from UFO sightings to the latest
"miracle" antiaging remedy.

In many ways, we live in exciting times. The speed at
which information is shared is amazing, and it allows us
to witness more about world issues and events than ever
before. Yet it seems what is real and true becomes more
and more of an elusion. Thanks to photo-enhancing

technology, we can't even always believe what we see in pictures. Leaders in marketing research tell us that putting the word *real*, *authentic*, or *honest* on a product will cause it to sell better because, as a society, we are desperate for what is real.

We are exposed to so much unreality that we're in danger of falling into the trap of seeking that which is unreal instead of what is real and true. Just because we bear the title of Christian doesn't mean we aren't susceptible to falsehoods. The Bible is full of warnings to God's people to pay attention and stay alert and to beware of false teachers. You see, even before television, radio, and the newspaper, lies existed. And even if we eliminated those information sources today, lies would continue.

Each of us at some point will buy a product based on statements we believe to be true, only to learn they were not; or believe in a politician only to discover later that his or her campaign was built on lies. These are disappointments, but likely little more. Other times the consequences of believing an untruth will be more serious. You might look at Hollywood glamour and be tempted to believe your life would be better if only . . . But be alert: life is rarely better or easier in someone else's backyard.

So how can you guard against believing the lies of the world? By keeping your life in line with the one real truth—God's teachings, not the world's. Guard yourself against deception by praying for wisdom and discernment. Read the Bible to fortify yourself with assurance of God's blessings. And keep your heart open to God's mercy and grace.

God's Reality Living—now that's a show I want to be on!

Think It

For the experienced to survive,
reality must be considered.
Charles B. Richardson

Live It

- Unsure about what's reality and what's a lie? Urban legends and Internet stories can be checked out online at www.snopes.com. You never again have to fall for manipulative lies or pass them on to others.

- Your source to unmasking lies the world tries to get you to believe is God's Word. Read a chapter of Proverbs each day this week as an antidote to the lies of the world.

- If your family loves watching reality TV, challenge them to your own personal reality "show." The goal is to live out the precepts of the Bible. Set up the rules together, based on God's Word. Live every day as if the world is watching—because in reality, it is!

40

Respect

Friends, we ask you to honor those leaders who work so hard for you, who have been given the responsibility of urging and guiding you along in your obedience. Overwhelm them with appreciation and love!
1 Thessalonians 5:12–13

Read It

Aretha Franklin put her unique voice behind the word *respect*, and it catapulted her to superstardom. You're probably humming it now or perhaps a few of you are belting out your best "shower" Aretha impersonation. "R-E-S-P-E-C-T. Find out what it means to me!"

But God had a few words to say about respect long before Aretha decided to sock it to us with her energetic rendition. God knows that respect is important in many areas of our lives. Think of the leaders He put into power in the Old Testament, such as Moses, Esther, and Solomon. In the New Testament we read of Paul, John the Baptist, and Peter, all chosen by God and given authority to act on His behalf. For God's plans to be carried out, His people need to respect those in authority—even though we realize they are not infallible.

As parents, it is our responsibility to teach our children to respect those in authority. Yet as our kids grow, they sometimes rebel against the very things we urged to love and respect. They, like us, will become more aware of what drives people to respect someone or something, and they might argue that respect is no longer warranted in some cases. This can cause problems in the family or at school. It will be important for you to point your children back to God's plan for their lives and to reinforce the principle that respect is the glue that holds communities—families, churches, and society as a whole—together.

R E-S-P-E-C-T. I know what it means to me. It means following God's plan and honoring those in authority by overwhelming them with appreciation and love.

Think It

Respect a man, he will do the more.
James Howell

Live It

- Remember to always speak respectfully of leaders—the president, your boss, your children's teachers, your pastor, etc.—especially in front of your children.

- Encourage your children to write a note or card expressing respect and appreciation to a leader.

- Don't let an opportunity go by without saying or doing something to "overwhelm" the authority figures in your life with love. Express thanks for their effort. Notice what they do well, and offer praise. Share some of the bounty of your kitchen or garden. Offer to help them when you see they could use a hand. Speak well of them to others. Send a card to brighten their day.

41

Self-Respect

*If you've gotten anything at all out of following Christ,
if his love has made any difference in your life, if being in
a community of the Spirit means anything to you, if you
have a heart, if you care—then do me a favor: Agree with
each other, love each other, be deep-spirited friends. Don't
push your way to the front; don't sweet-talk your way to
the top. Put yourself aside, and help others get ahead.
Don't be obsessed with getting your own advantage.
Forget yourselves long enough to lend a helping hand.*
Philippians 2:1–4

Read It

It's interesting that ever since the Baby Boomers were
dubbed, each generation feels entitled to a moniker of
its own. Generation Me or the Me Generation is used to
describe people born in the 1970s, 1980s, or 1990s. These
are today's young people—your children, maybe even you.
This generation was born at a time of peace, security, and
prosperity—with the result that duty or service to others
was not frequently required to supercede self-interest.
It's understandable, then, why many in this generation
believe their needs should come first.

But before you throw up your hands in despair, take
heart. This generation didn't adopt their way of thinking

because they're utterly selfish individuals without any hope of redemption. No, it has more to do with what our society has told them. They've grown up hearing mantras like "Be yourself," "Believe in yourself," and "You must love yourself first before you can love others."

The word *self-esteem* was not part of the parenting vocabulary before the 1970s. In previous generations, parents were responsible for many things concerning the care of their children, but positive self-esteem wasn't on the list. On the contrary, children were told not to think more highly of themselves than they should. My mom says she remembers twirling around in a beautiful dress and her grandmother telling her, not "You look like a movie star," as today's generation is likely to hear, but rather, "Pretty is as pretty does," stressing the value of character in the way we treat others.

I do believe the call for building healthy self-esteem has merit; but the way our society has taken this concept to an extreme bordering on self-worship is worrisome and works against God's plan for our lives.

Self-esteem is the collection of beliefs or feelings we have about ourselves—doesn't sound bad, does it? But here are the problems. First, the word *esteem* means to elevate positively and hold in high regard. Yet the Bible tells us to lay aside our selfish ambitions and be more concerned with helping others. That's the opposite of elevating ourselves to a position of high regard. The second problem is our expectation of others to simply hand out self-esteem to us like candy at a parade.

A better value to instill in our children is self-respect. Respecting oneself is not contingent on anything you do or anything others do for you. It is accepting yourself just as you are, not because of what you can or cannot do but because God made you as He chose to make you. As moms, we must rise to the challenge of making our children a sound counteroffer to what the world is teaching about self-esteem. Self-respect is that counteroffer. It isn't about gaining anything; it's about loving what we already have.

Think It

> Be yourself.
> Ape no greatness.
> Be willing to pass for what you are.
> Samuel Coley

Live It

- Ask your children what they like best about them- selves. If their responses include accomplishments or their appearance, you've got some work to do. Help them recognize that such things are fleeting, fade, or can be lost or forgotten. You may want to show them a picture of you at your coolest, when you were their age, as an object lesson on how looks, accomplishments, and fashions change and go out of style over time. Only what's inside stays the same and has real value. Explore the value each child has that comes from within—who they really are—and their value as children of God created in His image.

- Put coins worth 87¢ in an envelope (including lots of pennies) along with a folded slip of paper that says "87¢." Give each family member a slip of paper. Ask them to turn their backs (so no one else can see) and count the money, then write the amount of the change on their slip of paper so no one else can see it. Arrange turns so you can go second to last. When you count, remove one more penny, but still write "87¢" on your paper. After the last child has counted, go around the circle and have everyone announce the sum of money they counted. Pay particular attention to how the last child responds—whether he changes his total to go along with what everyone else has said, or whether he respects his counting ability enough to speak up about being a penny short. Use this as an illustration of being who we are and not succumbing to the pressure or expectations of others. When we look at what others are saying and doing, it's easy to feel shortchanged because we're not equal to their expectations. But help your kids see that we all are the way God made us—and that's enough.

- Read Romans 12:3–16 as a family, and discuss how it applies to everyday life. Help your kids see that when we respect ourselves and who God made us to be, we don't have to worry that associating with someone society deems "uncool" or "unworthy" will make us less than we are. Instead, it makes us bigger, better, stronger.

42

Service

*Work with a smile on your face, always keeping in mind
that no matter who happens to be giving the orders, you're
really serving God. Good work will get you good pay from
the Master, regardless of whether you are slave or free.*
Ephesians 6:7–8

Read It

Are you old enough to miss the full-service gas stations?
If you're a young mom, you may not even know what I'm
talking about. Let me tell you how it used to be. In the
good old days, when you pulled up to a gas station—which
was called a service station then—an attendant would
come right up to your window and ask, "Can I help you?"
You would say "Fill 'er up," meaning, please put gas in
my car until the pump stops. The attendant would start
the gas pumping and proceed to wash your windows and
check your oil while you waited comfortably inside your
car. After you paid for your gas, you might even receive
the station's free gift of the month—Christmas glass or
stamps to collect and cash in later. Oh, how I miss that
service!

Many such services have gone by the wayside as our
culture has gotten more fast paced. As a matter of fact,
our busy world has become our excuse for many instances

of not serving others. Yet the apostle Paul clearly points out in Ephesians 6 that any service to others is really service to God.

I love how Rick Warren puts it in his book *The Purpose-Driven Life*. He says it's not the duration of your life but the donation of your life that counts. How are you donating your life to others? Are you using your talents to bring God glory? Your children are depending on your example to show them what service to others really is.

Rick Warren also says to use your SHAPE—your Spiritual gifts, your Heart, your Abilities, your Personality, and your Experiences—to discover how you can best serve the kingdom of God. Not everyone is called to pulpit ministry, but everyone is called to minister in some way. How can you and your family be of service? Even though your children may never see a service-station attendant, be sure they see a service person in you.

Think It

To devote a portion of one's leisure to doing something for someone else is one of the highest forms of recreation.
Gerald B. Fitzgerald

Live It

- Have fun with a "secret buddy" game in your family. Randomly and secretly assign each member of the family another family member as his or her buddy. In the time frame you choose (a week, two weeks, or a month), the object is to find creative ways to serve that person and his or her needs while maintaining the secret of who is doing the serving.

- Adopt a family service project to serve your community, the needy, or some other appropriate group that could use help.

- Adopt a senior. Once a month, help or serve an elderly family member or shut-in from your neighborhood or church. Think of thoughtful ways to serve his or her needs.

- Write to thank a service member (or members) of our armed forces.

43

Sorrow

All praise to the God and Father of our Master,
Jesus the Messiah! Father of all mercy! God of all
healing counsel! He comes alongside us when we go
through hard times, and before you know it, he brings us
alongside someone else who is going through hard times
so that we can be there for that person just as God was
there for us. We have plenty of hard times that come from
following the Messiah, but no more so than the good times
of his healing comfort—we get a full measure of that, too.
2 Corinthians 1:3–5

Read It

I have dear friends who lost their son to suicide, another
special friend whose wife left him, and another who was
diagnosed with cancer—all during the Christmas season.
Sadness and sorrow know no holidays. Difficult times,
disappointments, mistakes are one thing; but the kind of
events I've just mentioned bring sorrow that saps us to
the core of our being and even challenges our faith.

Sorrow is deep distress, sadness, or regret, especially
for the loss of someone or something loved. Being a child
of God doesn't excuse us from the experiences in life that
bring deep sorrow. I wish that were the case, but it's not.
We live in a fallen world, where events happen that bring
us sadness. Perhaps you've lived through some of those

times—or are going through them right now. It is in those days that we especially have to keep our eyes on God.

When your children were babies and cried out in distress over being hungry or wet, do you remember how they would look to you for the help they needed? As a loving mother, you would look into their eyes and sense their needs with no verbal communication needed. God is our heavenly Father, and when we're in distress, if we will look to Him and keep our eyes on Him, He will hear and understand the cries of our hearts and will lovingly supply all that we need.

God knows the future—He knows exactly how He's going to bring you out of this on the other side. Keep your eyes on Him. Continue to put your trust in Him, and He will carry you through even the deepest sorrow.

Think It

There are times when God asks nothing of his children except silence, patience, and tears.
C. S. Robinson

Live It

- Read and pray Psalm 6, a song of sorrow. Can you relate? Pour out your hurt, your heart, and your sorrow to the Lord as you read these words aloud to Him.

- Keep a diary of your feelings through your days of sorrow. Looking back will help you be encouraged by how far you've come and the healing God is bringing to your life.

- Healing comes when we realize that our sorrow has produced good fruit. Read 2 Corinthians 1:3–5 again. Resolve not to avoid someone who is going through sorrow. Decide today to go "alongside" that person and "be there for that person just as God was there" for you. He or she will feel better, and so will you.

44

Strength

The moment I called out, you stepped in;
you made my life large with strength.
Psalm 138:3

Read It

When people think of the word *strength* or *power*, they often think of the power of a hurricane or perhaps a sumo wrestler. But if you've ever seen a tiny mom who, with the snap of a finger controls four kids, then you know what power really is!

Strength comes from having an inner confidence in one's ability to accomplish great things. On some days, your job as mom can sap your strength faster than a two-year-old can drain a sippy cup, and you begin to lose the confidence you once felt. Truth be told, on some days you probably want to let the kids take over the house while you curl up in the crib for a two-hour nap. Alas, that's not an option. God has entrusted you with caring for your children, and all kids need a mom who can stay strong in her resolve, convictions, and daily decisions. That's the mom trait that helps children feel safe and secure.

If you're feeling a little less than the muscle-mom you want to be, think of your mind and body as the electronic riding toy your children have. When the battery runs down, it just sits in the driveway, worthless to anyone until you push it up to the power source and plug it in. Once recharged, it's good to go for several days. Do you need to be recharged? We all do from time to time. Pull yourself up to the ultimate power source and plug in. God is even closer than the garage and easier to access than the charger you can never find when you need it.

Take a few moments today to close your eyes and let God fill you up with His power. Breathe deeply, and with each breath, be renewed and refreshed. Picture your body getting stronger and stronger until it's ready to zoom down the driveway. Your children are counting on you to be the strong mom God intends for you to be. You don't have to operate at hurricane strength every day, but you do need enough wind to help keep your "family boat" sailing smoothly.

Think It

*I've never been one
who thought the good Lord should make
life easy; I've just asked Him to make me strong.*
Eva Bowring

Live It

- Strengthen yourself physically. Plan a balanced regimen for yourself that includes regular exercise, proper nutrition, and adequate sleep. Like Daniel (Daniel 1:8–16), give yourself ten days to see how much stronger and healthier you feel.

- Strengthen yourself mentally and socially. You need adult, meaningful conversation that ranges wider than the walls of your home and your children. Learn something new. Sign up (with a friend) for a short class at the local community college. Join a book group. Do something to stretch your brain and exercise your fellowship muscles.

- Strengthen yourself spiritually. Develop a daily regimen of Bible reading, prayer, and devotions— quality time with God. It doesn't have to take long, but the time you invest will refresh and strengthen you for the day ahead.

45

Talents

*God's various gifts are handed out everywhere; but they
all originate in God's Spirit. God's various ministries are
carried out everywhere; but they all originate in God's
Spirit. God's various expressions of power are in action
everywhere; but God himself is behind it all. Each person
is given something to do that shows who God is: Everyone
gets in on it, everyone benefits. All kinds of things are
handed out by the Spirit, and to all kinds of people!*
1 Corinthians 12:4–6

Read It

My grandfather taught me the fine art of putting together
a puzzle—not those toddler puzzles that are made of wood
and have six pictures, each corresponding with a puzzle
piece. Those I can handle. I'm talking about a thousand-
piece puzzle. The kind you pour out on the table and then
stare at, wondering how those tiny pieces will ever look
like the picture on the box. It's puzzling for sure, but my
grandpa had the system down. I can still see him searching
for the corners, then the straight edges, all the while
explaining the importance of setting those pieces in place
first. "You have to frame the picture," he would say. "Then
you have to define the boundaries. Next, put all the pieces
in one area that have matching colors."

Do you realize how much life is like a large puzzle? There are thousands of pieces to put together to form the magnificent picture of our existence. And if life is like a puzzle, then we must realize that each of us is just one tiny piece of it. Still, anyone who has nearly completed a puzzle and discovered one piece missing will tell you that no piece is unimportant—it takes every one of them to complete the picture.

God sees the puzzle of our lives as it looks completed. He already knows where you fit in. As a matter of fact, He has equipped you for a perfect fit.

Are you still not sure where you fit in? What your purpose is? Well, use Grandpa's tricks. Find your corners first: God says your purpose in life should be to serve Him and others. Those are great anchors. Next, locate your boundaries. Perhaps those are your family, your church, your work, or your community. Now look for matching "colors"—in other words, look for areas to serve that match the God-given talents you have.

Remember that in God's masterpiece, no one is left out. Using these simple steps and some patience, you will be well on your way to finding where you fit—and before you know it, a beautiful picture will develop.

Think It

Hide not your talents, they for use were made.
What's a sundial in the shade?
Benjamin Franklin

Live It

- Google *aptitude test* and *spiritual gifts test*. Choose one (or one of each), fill out the questionnaire, and analyze the results. Does anything surprise you? What are your strengths? Does it give you any new ideas as to where you might want to focus your God-given talents?

- Once you've identified your talents and special gifts, spend some time considering how to use those unique gifts in a way all your own to be the best mother for your kids. Are you creative? Inspiring? Humorous? Organized? Sensitive? How can you capitalize on these gifts to be an outstanding mother? How can you capitalize on your gifts in serving others (school, church, job, community)?

- Help your kids identify and appreciate their talents and special aptitudes. Make them feel safe to be different from their siblings and friends and to chart a course that uses their gifts and interests most fully.

46

Training

Point your kids in the right direction—
when they're old they won't be lost.
Proverbs 22:6

Read It

When my son was around eighteen months old, he began throwing the most awful temper tantrums. I remember calling my mom in despair and in search of answers. Why would a perfectly normal toddler start throwing such fits? In hindsight, it's clear that I had already answered my own question—because he was a perfectly normal toddler.

It's normal for little ones to get frustrated with life as they seek to master new skills but aren't equipped to handle them yet. However, even though toddlers and tantrums go together like peanut butter and jelly, it wasn't a behavior I was going to allow. Mom's advice to ignore the fit but remain firm and calm as I went about my chores proved effective, and soon my foot-stomping, screaming boy got past that stage.

While techniques vary, the common goal is to train our kids to behave appropriately. As tired, frazzled moms, we're often tempted to stomp our feet and scream a little ourselves, especially when our children display undesirable behavior. And sometimes we fall into the trap of accepting responsibility for their behavior instead of their training.

But training your youngster to behave appropriately is one of the greatest gifts you can give. It prepares him or her to fashion a future filled with more joy than trouble. Yes, the job is challenging. Your parenting skills—and your patience—will be tested every day. How your children see you respond to their behavior, both good and bad, is part of training them to become the men and women God wants them to be. Training requires calm, consistent behavior from the trainer. If you see that your child needs more training in some area, step up to the plate and do the right thing. Train today for a better tomorrow!

Think It

In early childhood you may lay the foundation
of poverty or riches, industry or idleness, good or evil,
by the habits to which you train your children.
Teach them right habits then, and their future is safe.
Lydia Sigourney

Live It

- Think about it: What one (or more) behavior or attitude do you want your children to learn? What must you do to train them to master that? Make a plan and stick with it. Consistency is the key.

- While you don't want to be a nitpicking perfectionist who crushes your children's spirits, you do want to help them set good patterns that will last a lifetime. Give yourself permission to correct your children's grammar, table manners, spelling, posture, gum chewing, nose picking, sarcastic tone, or whatever it is that might not look so good on them as adults.

- What bad habit as a mom do you need to train yourself to overcome? How will you do that this week?

47

Understanding

*We all live off his generous bounty, gift after gift
after gift. We got the basics from Moses, and then this
exuberant giving and receiving, this endless knowing and
understanding—all this came through Jesus, the Messiah.
No one has ever seen God, not so much as a glimpse. This
one-of-a-kind God-Expression, who exists at the very
heart of the Father, has made him plain as day.*

John 1:16–18

Read It

"You don't understand" is the battle cry of many preteens
and teens as they struggle to find their place in the world.
It baffles us moms to be so suddenly downgraded from
a virtual encyclopedia of knowledge to a mere babbling
grown-up who's too old and out of touch to relate to a
hip teen.

A defiant child who either mutters those words under
his breath or yells them at the top of his lungs is really
saying "You don't know me." And the answer would be
"You're right, I don't know you." Teens become someone
they have never been before. They grow and change daily,
both physically and emotionally, making it hard enough
for them to keep up with who they are, not to mention
the rest of us who try to live with them.

But maybe teens aren't the only ones who feel this

angst. How about you? Do you ever cry out to God that He just doesn't understand? Thomas Edison noted that the concept of understanding comes from the simple words *under* and *stand*. He said that one must be willing to "stand under" someone in order to be receptive to obtaining and retaining information from that person. Edison's point was that if people would just lower themselves a little and be willing to accept the ideas and opinions of others, a lot more understanding would take place.

Teens don't think we understand them because we have a tough time "standing under" their ideas and opinions. We want them to accept what we say to them, not the other way around. Generally, that concept and our motives are good. We've been there, done that, and we don't want our kids to make the same mistakes we did. But God allows us to make mistakes, doesn't He? And God also understands us completely.

As I read Edison's explanation, a lightbulb went on in my head (Thomas would be so proud). It hit me that Jesus lowered himself from the right hand of God to walk among us humans. That's how God is capable of understanding our every want, need, fear, concern, and all the other desires of our hearts. He was willing to "stand under" us—to walk among us, to get to know us, and even to serve us.

As you work on your relationship with your teens, remember how God came as a man in order to identify with us—to understand us—and be willing to "stand down" enough to listen to what your teen is really trying to say.

Think It

Nothing in life is to be feared. It is only to be understood.
Marie Curie

Live It

- Reverse roles as you play out one of the common debates from your household. For instance, you might argue the point of a teen wanting more freedom, and your teen might express the concerns of a parent. Try to honestly see the other side and argue it as convincingly and kindly as you would your own. At the end, discuss how it made you feel. Do you think you understand each other better?

- When it's just a matter of preference and not principle or safety, be willing to accede to your teens' (or children's) wishes from time to time. Ask them to return the favor to you occasionally, even when they don't understand where you're coming from.

- Read 1 Corinthians 13:11–12. When you or your child is feeling misunderstood, remember that promise and rejoice. Someday we will both know and be known fully.

48

Unity

May our dependably steady and warmly
personal God develop maturity in you so that you
get along with each other as well as Jesus gets along
with us all. Then we'll be a choir—not our voices only, .
but our very lives singing in harmony in a stunning
anthem to the God and Father of our Master Jesus!
Romans 15:5–6

Read It

I recently attended a school Christmas program that included the sweet sound of children's voices singing carols. Well, the sound was almost sweet. One small boy in row three was offering up notes that don't appear anywhere on a piano scale. There was no mistaking who the singing-challenged child was—not noticing he wasn't on the same pitch as the other students, he sang with gusto. At the end of the performance, the audience smiled and clapped loudly. No one would dream of saying anything other than "Bravo!" to every child in the program.

Had this been a choral group of grown-ups, I can promise you, the applause would not have been so generous. What we accept from children is one thing; what we accept from mature adults is another. And that's as it should be. As we grow and mature, more is expected of us. I love to sing and rarely miss an opportunity to join a choir. I do not have an excellent solo voice or perfect pitch, though I can tell when a choir is supposed to be in unison but isn't. Unison is when each member sings the exact same note so that the effect is of one unified voice. For vocal unity to take place, every singer must listen carefully to their own voice and the voices of those around them to ensure that all the notes are the same. They must be content not to stand out but rather to be a valuable member of a team that, when working together, makes a beautiful sound.

The model for singing in unison is one we should look to for all of our relationships, whether it's with our spouses, our siblings, our church family, or our coworkers. Working together requires maturity and being content to not always be the center of attention. It calls for more than just not causing problems; it means cooperating proactively. To do that, we have to listen to ourselves and to the others around us. When we notice that we're no longer in tune with them, it's time to figure out why and what we can do to improve the relationship.

Unity in song and in life doesn't mean you don't have your own voice; it just means that you choose to join in with those around you to make one beautiful sound.

Think It

Unity is strength . . .
when there is teamwork and
collaboration, wonderful things can be achieved.
Mattie Stepanek

Live It

- As a family, sing a song in unison. Can you do it? Working—or singing—together takes practice.

- Tackle a household project together. Praise and congratulate your children when you see them working together. Remind them of the importance of unity when trying to accomplish any task.

- Play this simple game as a family. For each round, list five categories (for example: music groups, favorite foods, vacation spots, colors, and past presidents). Each person should write down one item that fits each category (like the Beatles, pizza, Niagara Falls, purple, and Abraham Lincoln). The entire family gets a point only when all answers in any category are the same. As you play, you'll get better at anticipating others' answers, adjusting, and responding in unity. It's great practice.

Victory

49

*Do you see what this means—all these pioneers
who blazed the way, all these veterans cheering us on?
It means we'd better get on with it. Strip down, start
running—and never quit! No extra spiritual fat, no
parasitic sins. Keep your eyes on Jesus, who both began
and finished this race we're in. Study how he did it.
Because he never lost sight of where he was headed—that
exhilarating finish in and with God—he could put up
with anything along the way: Cross, shame, whatever.
And now he's there, in the place of honor, right alongside
God. When you find yourselves flagging in your faith,
go over that story again, item by item, that long
litany of hostility he plowed through. That will
shoot adrenaline into your souls!*

Hebrews 12:1–3

Read It

Ashley was excited. It was the state track meet. She was
poised at the starting block, ready to run the hundred-
meter hurdles. By all accounts, she was expected to win
this race. The gun fired and Ashley darted from her block,
only to be called back because of an error in her stance.
She had run hurdles for her team for the past two years,
and her stance had never been challenged. She shook

it off and placed her feet back in the blocks. Again the sound of the gun pierced the air, but again the girls were called back.

Trying to stay calm, Ashley walked it off and adjusted her stance according to the instructions of the judge. By that time you could hear a pin drop in the university stadium where the meet was held. The next sound of the gun made the spectators jump, but the race was finally underway. Ashley cleared the first two hurdles with ease, but by the third hurdle it was evident that her timing was off. On the fourth hurdle, she went down. The crowd gasped in horror as her body hit the ground. The other runners glided past her.

But Ashley didn't stay down. What a proud mom I was as I watched her get up and limp to the finish line. Her knee was bleeding and her hands were bruised, but she had come to the meet that day to finish the race, and that's what she was going to do.

Victory comes in many packages. For some, it's first place without a scratch. For others, it's just finishing, broken and bruised, but victorious nonetheless. Moms, you are running a marathon. Being a mother is a hard job, and sometimes the rewards seem few and far between. But God has called you to this job of caring for and nurturing your children, and I believe He has a special place in heaven for mommies. Maybe it will be a room with a white couch that never gets dirty, a tall glass of lemonade with no fingerprints on it, and all the magazines you never got to read. But I'm guessing it'll be bigger and better than anything we can imagine.

So on those days when you've tripped and fallen, pick yourself up and limp on toward the finish line. In God's record book, finishing well is a victory indeed.

Think It

> *Victories that are easy are cheap.*
> *Those only are worth having*
> *which come as the result of hard work.*
> Henry Ward Beecher

Live It

- Think of someone you know (or knew) who is (or was) an example of victorious living. What makes that person worthy of your admiration? What can you learn from him or her and apply to your own life?

- Take inventory of some of your past victories. Allow them to inspire and encourage you now and for the future.

- Celebrate the victories in your life. Set goals, and when you reach them, give yourself a special treat, a day off, or a pat on the back.

50

Wisdom

God answered Solomon, "This is what has come out
of your heart: You didn't grasp for money, wealth, fame,
and the doom of your enemies; you didn't even ask for a
long life. You asked for wisdom and knowledge so you could
govern well my people over whom I've made you king.
Because of this, you get what you asked for—wisdom and
knowledge. And I'm presenting you the rest as a bonus—
money, wealth, and fame beyond anything the
kings before or after you had or will have."
2 Chronicles 1:11–12

Read It

I once heard a comedienne joke that each time a mom
gives birth to a child, she loses valuable brain cells. I'm not
sure how scientifically accurate that is, but I do remember
many nights rocking my colicky baby when I felt like my
brain had turned the consistency of baby cereal. In the
first few months of our children's lives, being wise is not
a top priority—getting sleep is. Then they grow up, and
you find yourself willing to trade two hours of sleep for
two minutes of clarity and wisdom. Oh, to be back in the
baby stage, when you were exhausted but the questions
and answers were simple.

One definition of wisdom is making the best use of

available knowledge. That makes me think of the wise king Solomon and how he gathered information in order to make wise decisions. Guess what? You can do that too!

If you've ever listened to Dr. Laura Schlessinger on the radio, you've likely heard her frequent challenge to "go out and do the right thing." She says that because she knows that people usually do know what the right thing is. God doesn't keep wisdom hidden from us. He's not some sadistic schoolteacher who purposely leaves out a page of the study guide. God wants us to be wise. He gave Solomon wisdom simply because he asked for it!

Confucius once said that wisdom can be learned by three methods: reflection, the noblest according to him; imitation, which he thought was the easiest; and experience, which he deemed the hardest. I agree with Confucius, except I would say the first and best method is prayer. If you feel like you don't have the answers, pray. Ask God for the wisdom you need to make the right decisions. He gave it to Solomon, and He'll give it to you too.

Think It

*Make wisdom your provision
for the journey from youth to old age,
for it is a more certain support
than all other possessions.*
Diogenes Laërtius

Live It

- Read James 1:5. Ask God for wisdom right now—and whenever you feel confused.

- You do have wisdom, maybe more than you realize. Some of it has been passed on for generations. Write down the wise sayings you learned from your grandparents and parents. How many of these do you repeat to your kids? Now consider what wise words you pass on to your children from your own experience. If you need help, ask your kids. They've been listening and know your wise sayings as well as you know those of your parents. Way to go, Mom!

- If you feel that you lack wisdom in a particular area in dealing with your family, put some time and effort into finding wise advice. Consult the Bible, Christian parenting books, and other trustworthy sources. You'll know you have wise advice when it resonates with what you know in your heart is right through God's Spirit.

51

Worry

Has anyone by fussing before the mirror ever gotten taller
by so much as an inch? If fussing can't even do that, why
fuss at all? Walk into the fields and look at the wildflowers.
They don't fuss with their appearance—but have you ever
seen color and design quite like it? The ten best-dressed
men and women in the country look shabby alongside
them. If God gives such attention to the wildflowers,
most of them never even seen, don't you think he'll
attend to you, take pride in you, do his best for you?
Luke 12:25–28

Read It

When I was young, my mother used to call me a
worrywart. I wasn't sure what the "wart" part meant,
but I was all too familiar with worry. Even as a youngster
in elementary school, I worried—that I wouldn't get
picked for a team at recess, that I hadn't studied enough,
that my parents would get a divorce. When I got older,
I attended a Christian youth camp and discovered this
passage in Luke 12. Then I worried that I worried too
much! I seemed destined to a life of wringing my hands
and pacing the floor.

But when I had my first child, I decided it was time
to digest this verse instead of just chewing on it. I read

and reread it, and soon it became clear to me that God was absolutely in control. I put myself in God's place and realized how sad I would be if my child didn't trust me to take care of him or her. I would be devastated to know that any of my children went to bed at night doubting my ability to care for their needs.

You see, worrying says one of three things to God. Either we think He's unconcerned, unaware, or unprepared. None of these characteristics are true of our God. Since God loves us so much that He sent His only Son to save us, I don't believe He is unconcerned about us now. The Bible tells us that God knows every hair on our head, so I'm quite sure He's aware of all the anxieties we have. And He has already experienced every kind of suffering known to mankind, so I have no doubt that He is prepared to handle my cares and concerns.

Are you a worrier, like I was? As a recovering worrier, let me give you some advice. Sit down with this passage from Luke and spend some quality time with it. Don't just chew on it, swallow it and use the strength from it to grow. Also, chew on these facts: 40 percent of things we worry about never happen; 30 percent are unchangeable deeds of the past; 12 percent focus on others' opinions, again beyond our power to change; 10 percent center on health, which can get worse with worry; only 8 percent contain a real problem with a possible solution by you. According to this, 92 percent of our worries are needless!

Actually, 100 percent are needless, because God can handle them all. So stop worrying. You have nothing to lose and everything to gain by turning your troubles over to the Lord.

Think It

Worry a little bit every day and in a lifetime you will lose a couple of years. If something is wrong, fix it if you can. But train yourself not to worry. Worry never fixes anything.
Mary Hemingway

Live It

- Worries and fears are contagious. If you don't want your children to be fearful worriers, it's up to you to set the example. Express confidence and trust in God rather than sharing your worry and doubt.

- Write your worries on a piece of paper. Pray, committing these to God. Then burn (be careful, but don't worry about burning down the house), shred, or otherwise destroy your list of worries. Now leave the "worrying" to God.

- Read Philippians 4:6–8. Make it your standard for living. Guard your mind and heart. Steer your thoughts away from the negative or worrisome and onto the positive.

52

You

*I'll show up and take care of you as I promised
and bring you back home. I know what I'm doing.
I have it all planned out—plans to take care of you, not
abandon you, plans to give you the future you hope for.*
Jeremiah 29:10–11

Read It

When my oldest grandson, John Luke, was eight years old, he and his three younger siblings were visiting and spending the night with me. It was a Saturday night with church the next day, so it had been a particularly busy evening with the younger children needing most of my attention. I had fixed supper, given baths, brushed teeth, read books, and chased kids all evening, but John Luke, being older, hadn't required much from me. At some point I sent him to take a shower and brush his teeth while I tucked in the little ones for the night. Once I got the kids in bed, I went to the kitchen to clean up.

After a while, John Luke came in, gave me a hug, and went to bed on his own. I did a few more things and then collapsed for the night myself.

The next morning I got up early and went straight to the shower. When I opened the door, there awaited the best surprise I've ever received. In huge letters on the wall of the shower, John Luke had written with a crayon soap: "I Love You, 2-Mama."

That gift of love from John Luke struck me as a beautiful illustration of what God does for us every day. First, John Luke *planned* this surprise for me. He thought about me and my needs. Jeremiah 29:11 says that God has "plans to take care of you, not abandon you, plans to give you the future you hope for." He thinks about you individually and has crafted a wonderful plan specifically for you.

The next thing John Luke did was *perform* what he had planned. If he had thought about it but never put it into an action, even if he had told me about the plan, it wouldn't have had the same effect. God doesn't just have plans for you; He is actively working to make those plans become true. In Jeremiah God tells the people, "I'll show up and take care of you as I promised."

And finally, John Luke *patiently waited*. His patience came from his desire for me to get the most out of the experience—he closed his eyes that night knowing that I was going to get an amazing surprise the next morning. Have you noticed that God is patient with you? But how patient are you with God? Have you ever prayed for something and really wanted to add the word *now* to the end of your prayer? I have. We have a tendancy to want what we want when we want it. But God's timing is perfect, and He wants you to get the most out of what He has in store for you. So He is willing to patiently wait for the perfect time to carry out those plans. Are you willing to wait for Him?

As you go about your busy life, be thankful for God's good plans for you, for His faithfulness in performing those plans in your life, and for His merciful patience as He shapes you into the godly woman and mom you desire to be.

Think It

God deals with us whether in sickness or in health, whether in prosperity or adversity, whether in good or in evil days, whether in life or in death, not according to our merit but according to His mercy and love.

Albert J. Penner

Live It

- Write out the words of Jeremiah 29:11 on a note card or sticky note and post it where you will see it daily. Rejoice in the knowledge that God has good plans for you.

- Think back to the best, most elaborate plan you've ever planned, performed, and waited patiently to maximize the results for someone you loved. Why did you do it? How did it make you feel? Now imagine: God, who loves you with a love far beyond even the strongest human love, is doing the same thing for you daily. How does that make you feel?

- Celebrate you. God loves you; that's enough to make you worthy of celebrating. Do something rewarding, fun, spur-of-the-moment just for you. Get the hot fudge sundae, spend time at the spa, relax in a bubble bath with a good book, get a new hairstyle, or dump the pot roast and make reservations at that fancy restaurant you'd love to try. Enjoy!

About the Author

Holding a degree in elementary education, Chrys volunteered her time for over ten years teaching children with learning differences as well as directing a Christian youth camp for nearly twenty years. She is the recipient of the JC Penney Golden Rule Award for Volunteer Services and has been named among the Who's Who of American Teachers. Currently, Chrys speaks to women's groups and teaches a young adult class at her local church. An avid tennis player, she is a three-time state champion and has played in regional and national tournaments. She is a senior editor and the creative director for Howard Books, where she is responsible for the design of all book covers and producing gift books. She is also an avid photographer whose photographs have appeared over twenty books. She had edited and co-written over fifty books and is the author of seven books that have sold over a million copies in five languages. She received a Silver Angel Award from the Hollywood-based Excellence in Media organization for her works of outstanding moral, ethical, and social impact on America. Chrys Howard lives in West Monroe, Louisiana, with her husband, John. They have three grown children and ten grandchildren.